Holistic Data Governance

Volume I:
The Guardrail Hierarchy

Dr David Kowalski

Technics Publications
SEDONA, ARIZONA

115 Linda Vista, Sedona, AZ 86336 USA
https://www.TechnicsPub.com

Edited by Sadie Hoberman

Cover design by Lorena Molinari

First Printing 2024

Copyright © 2024 by Dr David Kowalski

ISBN, print ed.   9781634625661
ISBN, Kindle ed.   9781634625678
ISBN, PDF ed.   9781634625685

Library of Congress Control Number: 2024946258

Endorsements

Data Governance can be complicated and difficult (and as David reiterates, specific to each organization). This short text provides guardrails that should help most practitioners with the challenging task of getting organized. I plan to keep a copy handy as I recommend all organizations do. Getting started is perhaps the most important part of this process and this book provides an excellent foundation.

Peter Aiken, data management thought leader and author of several bestsellers, including *The CDO Journey. He is the Founding Director, Anything Awesome LLC*

As I was reading the book, my neurons were firing on all cylinders with my inner voice saying, "I wish I had this book when I was starting out as a Data Governance practitioner". It communicates the value of the work that we do and the positive impacts we can bring to our stakeholders and the broader Community. Whether you are just starting out as a Data Governance professional or are a seasoned practitioner. If you're in the C-Suite or, in fact, any stakeholder in a Data Governance organization, David's book can serve as a practical framework for creating and executing the Data Governance agenda in your organization. There is a lifetime of experience in these pages, and I would commend this book to become a part of your Data Governance toolkit.

Andrew Andrews, Vice President Marketing, DAMA International & Regional Advocate, Australia and New Zealand, Enterprise Data Management Council.

If you are "doing" (or thinking about doing) data governance, you need this book! David lays out a compelling approach for his "Guardrail Hierarchy," which covers what documents you need to make data governance work and why. Remember that documents are not just files. They represent the essential thinking, direction, and actions for an organization to get the most from their data assets. Use this straightforward, easy-to-digest book as a practical guide for your work.

Danette McGilvray, President and Principle, Granite Falls Consulting, Inc. Known for her Ten Steps™ approach to data quality which has been embraced as a proven method for creating, managing, and sustaining high-quality data in any organization. She is the author of the book *Executing Data Quality Projects: Ten Steps to Quality Data and Trusted Information*™, 2nd Ed. (Elsevier/Academic Press, 2021).

Everyone's organization has a common need: to effectively use its data. And, to produce instructions about the who-what-when- where-why-how's of governing, managing and using that data. But what type of instructions? What type of documents? What's enough, and what is too much? Isn't this why you've picked up this book? Because you're caught in the space between "Doesn't everyone know this already..." and "Well I guess we need to spell this out, print this out, and make them read it." David reminds us that everyone's organization has its own culture, expectations, and attitudes toward documentation. He's also outlined a hierarchical way of thinking about, classifying, and deciding what data-related policies and other guardrails should contain. His system is a really good starting point for deciding what's right for you.

Gwen Thomas, Founder of the Data Governance Institute

Having spent years in the trenches of Data Governance, I can tell you firsthand that the foundation of any successful program is built on essential guardrails—those critical documents and principles that guide every decision and action. In 'Holistic Data Governance™,' David Kowalski brings these crucial elements into sharp focus. This book isn't just a guide; it's a complete overview of the guardrails needed for a sustainable data governance framework. David doesn't just offer theory; he shares practical examples on how to put these guardrails into action. His insights are invaluable, practical, and directly applicable—a must-read for every data governance practitioner.

Mathias Vercauteren, The Data Governance Advocate & President of Data Vantage Consulting

David Kowalski's "Holistic Data Governance™: Volume I - The Guardrail Hierarchy" transcends theoretical discussions by providing real-world anecdotes and practical recommendations to establish effective and cohesive data management and governance strategies. His "Guardrails" is a compelling blend of insight, practicality, and expertise ---a must-read for every data professional seeking sustainable data governance.

Robert Wentz, Senior Advisor, EDM Council

Contents

Figures

Tables

Foreword

There was a warm San Diego breeze, the smell of good food, and the laughter of colleagues and friends. David and I had joined others for a meal at the end of a great conference day. Of course, our conversation focused on music composition and how "thinking in music" translates to "thinking in data." It can be so energizing when surrounded by others who get excited by the same ideas and challenges. Then there was a lull, and David sighed. "I'm thinking of writing a book," he said quietly, "but...."

I commiserated silently. Those of us who think for a living – and teach, design programs, and coach – we're always writing. But getting a big book out...**that** can be something else. Especially when you work in a multi-faceted field like Data Governance. It's a lot.

"Just do it," I finally said. "Aim for something smaller, a bounded discussion that won't take on a life of its own...maybe 100 pages or so."

David's face lit up. "What are you thinking of?" I asked. "Quick – you've got three minutes. What needs to be said?"

Maybe we spent a few minutes more than three, and maybe this book has a few pages more than a hundred. But before our entrees arrived, David had shared his common-sense approach to communicating the who-what-when-where-why-hows of capturing the types of instructions that organizations need as part of their Data Governance initiatives. He outlined a hierarchical way of classifying them and describing what they should contain.

Without props, paper, or pencil, he made that cascading logic come alive. "Sounds like a book," I said. "Just do it!"

And he did. I've been privileged to read drafts. And privileged to debate a point or two, such as whether a specific document in his Guardrail Hierarchy should sit above or below another. To jump between "thinking about doing" and "thinking about thinking." To discuss what "goes without saying" versus what "really needs to be said."

Because, after all, isn't that why you've picked up this book? Aren't you caught in the space between "Doesn't everyone know this already?" and "Well, I guess we need to spell this out, print this out, and make them read it."

And you've likely had your own quiet moments of contemplation. How many pages are too many? Too few? How do we reconcile strategic instructions with targeted details? How do we convey that all the details are branches of a few really important decisions that have been made?

As David reminds us, everyone's organization has its own culture, expectations, and attitudes toward documentation. But they all share a common need: to use their data effectively. Decisions and directions must be established. They must be captured. They must make sense to all who participate in managing, governing, and using data.

I hope this book helps you think through the hierarchical nature of governance documentation. I hope it helps you design the set that makes sense for you.

And, I hope you find this type of work as much fun as David and I do.

Gwen

Gwen Thomas
Founder of the Data Governance Institute

How to Use this Book

There's no *one right way* to define your Data Governance Guardrails, but this book aims to establish a coherent, integrated approach to building out a set of Guardrail documents that work *as a whole*...documents that reinforce one another with common themes that focus on achieving what I call *Holistic Data Governance*™. This is an approach to Data Governance that respects the localized needs of the individual parts of your organization while orchestrating them into a meaningful whole that helps deliver the data that your organization needs at all levels in order to make meaningful decisions about how to succeed in your particular industry.

Ideally, you'll read this book from beginning to end, but if you don't have time, start with the Introduction and the first four chapters, which will give you a strong basis for understanding the concepts that drive Holistic Data Governance. From there, you can jump to the chapters relevant to those types of Guardrail documents that are of most importance to you, whether they are Strategic, Governance, or Execution in nature. The key "connective tissue" (the concepts that tie each document to one or more of the others) appears in each relevant place, and you can always jump around if you feel so inclined. Terminology is generally defined at its first appearance, so you may miss the formal definition if you jump around like this, but you can always consult the Glossary for clarification. Additionally, the Appendices offer some high-level summaries of the material to allow you to take in everything at a glance.

Since this is a book about Data Governance Guardrails, it seems only appropriate to place certain guideposts along the way. To help guide you through the material, you'll notice the following "callouts" to supplement the main text.

1. **Tales from the Trenches.** To help dispel any notion that this is a theoretical construct with a limited basis in practical reality, I will periodically recount actual "tales from the trenches" to help relate the concepts discussed in the text to some of the real-world problems that gave rise to those concepts in the first place. These will appear in a framed box as follows:

    > This is what REALLY happened...

2. **Calling Out Cultural Considerations.** No two companies are identical, and there is no "one size fits all" for this material. Most of the concepts expressed herein can be adapted to many different types of industries, both large and small, and across sectors (public, private, non-profit, etc.). Where I feel there is a strong likelihood of some kind of cultural difference arising, I have highlighted this material with a "Cultural Difference" icon:

3. **Glossary.** Finally, all terms that have a potential for ambiguity or that could be expected not to be immediately familiar are defined at their first point of usage. This is usually done in the body of the text but is occasionally relegated to a footnote if that better preserves the flow. Additionally, all such terms appear in the Glossary at the end of the book.

Introduction

We've all heard the numbers. Data production is increasing at an exponential rate. Big Data has become Humongous Data and the pace of data creation shows no signs of slowing down. Obviously, none of us has to deal with ALL that data but the pattern is clear: the more our business focuses on leveraging the *value* inherent in our data, the more data we need to manage.

How do we manage that data? We start by knowing and documenting what is important to the organization and what is, therefore, important about the data itself. We look at the processes for using, managing, and governing it. We also create high-level strategic instructions, which inform more detailed documents. Together, this forms a hierarchy of documents, and it is this hierarchy that is the primary subject of this book.

Of course, getting value from data takes more than instructions. The book touches on technology, people, processes, culture, and more. But we'll look at them through dual lenses:

- Governance – who creates and issues the instructions, to whom and what they apply, and ensuring they work together to achieve a "holistic" approach to Data Management.

- Guardrail documents – the hierarchy of instructions that we encapsulate as formal documentation to guide us to an effective, holistic approach to our data.

While technologists continue to create more and more tools to help manage this endless onslaught of incoming data, we must not lose sight of the key *fundamentals* of Data Management/Data Governance. This is **not** a sexy conversation. It's not a bright, shiny object to dazzle your decision-makers, but it amounts to BASIC COMMON SENSE...Common Sense that is all too often lacking in Data Management organizations. When we bask in the glitter of all the new "toys" at our disposal, it is easy to lose sight of these fundamentals, and, as a result, we end up with lots of garbage created very quickly.

That's not to say that the new technology is without value–far from it. But to put that new technology in context, let's draw an analogy with building a new house. You can have a fabulous layout of rooms, with beautiful fittings and an exterior with dazzling curb appeal. But if you put all of that on top of an inadequately designed foundation, your dream house, if you can build it at all, will rapidly come tumbling down into a pile of rubble.

Obviously, your organization is only responsible for producing and managing a fraction of the unimaginably huge amount of global data but a tiny fraction of Humongous Data is still a *lot* of data! To make so much diverse data widely available while maintaining quality, Data Management must be able to orchestrate at scale. In part, that means assembling a diverse set of skills and resources across your organization. It can seem like an insurmountable challenge to manage the quality and accessibility of so much data. It becomes even more onerous when you realize the importance of maintaining **trust** in that data without burning out your staff. You have to collect the data, document it, tie it to meaningful metadata, and catalog it–AND you have to do it in a timely manner! For most large companies, that means automating much of the work, but even companies with more modest data needs risk overwhelming their staff with the demands of their data.

Whether you are automating a high degree of your data management or still relying on a mix of humans and machines to accomplish the work, the best way to leverage your resources is to get everyone rowing in the same direction or marching to the same drummer–pick the metaphor of your choice. To do that, you need a common set of directions. To ensure that your Data Management practice is reliable, consistent, and repeatable, you must Document, Approve, Publish, and Enforce those directions.

Figure 1: The Guardrail Lifecycle

That sequence is quite significant, and I especially want to underscore that I've placed "Documented" at the base of that pyramid. A fundamental rule of any kind of Data Governance Guardrail is that "if it's not written down, it doesn't exist!" That may sound obvious, yet I have seen countless cases throughout my career of Strategies, Policies, Standards, and Processes that are left completely undocumented or, if they *are* documented, the documentation is lacking in some way or another. In a world of crowd-sourcing and letting generative AI do your thinking for you...where there's a feeling that by the time you document a guardrail, it's already obsolete, it is more important than ever to underscore the importance of having clear, unambiguous Data Governance Guardrails. The more unambiguously these guardrails are documented and the more you integrate them across your organization, the easier it is to standardize how to do things.

Know Your Internal Protocols

This is a book about Data Governance, but it is also a book about publishing. More specifically, it's a book about publishing the documents that will impart direction, structure, and control over your Data Governance and Data Management initiatives. The crafting of effective Data Governance Guardrails obviously requires a thorough knowledge of what is required of the Data Governance organization in general, as well as what is required of Data Governance *at your organization*. But, beyond this Subject Matter Expertise, you also need the same kinds of resources that any publishing house needs.

First and foremost, you need good writers. No matter how knowledgeable your Subject Matter Experts (SMEs) may be, their expertise is meaningless if they can't communicate it clearly and effectively to the rest of the organization. It's unrealistic to presuppose that because the SME's *know* the material, they can *teach* it. Maybe they can, but it's equally likely that you'll need to partner them up with in-house "ghost writers" (or hire the authorial expertise of a third-party documentation company). Wherever they come from, you can't shortcut this step.

You also need to understand the styles, mandates, and constraints of your in-house documentation, as well as your organization's document publishing protocols and standards. These will dictate everything from document formats to official vetting and approval processes. In particular, the vetting and approval process may have significantly different paths depending on the document under consideration. The designation of something as a Policy, a Plan, a Guideline, a Directive, or any of a dozen other document types will often imply a particular approval method for that particular designation. Absent a comprehensive knowledge of such standards, you risk, at best, extensive reworking of your documents and, at worst, outright rejection of your work.

Why We Need Guardrails

Guardrails keep us safe and define expectations.

If the phrase "Data Governance Guardrail" is new to you, let's think about it in much the same way as we think about the guardrails that exist (or *don't* exist!) by the side of a roadway—especially a twisty, windy mountain roadway where a slight deviation from your intended course can be disastrous.

Figure 2: Guardrails keep us safe

Sometimes the safety barriers will be supplemented by warning signs (e.g., "Blind Curve Ahead"). These work together with the physical barriers to prepare drivers for conditions where specific behaviors are needed to ensure everyone's safety. Much like the guardrails on these highly exposed roads, a Data Governance Guardrail helps keep everyone on a safe course.

> *Roadway guardrails consist of stone or steel, but a Data Governance guardrail contains words—carefully chosen words, clearly articulated, which direct the behaviors of your individual Data Management practitioners along the roadways on which you intend them to travel.*

To translate that into more specific terms, we will use the term, "Data Governance Guardrail" (or, simply, "Guardrail") to refer to any document that we use to direct, mandate, guide, or control the implementation and operations of Data and Data Management-related practices. This integrated mesh of strategies, policies, standards, process definitions, and various execution plans constitutes our organization-wide Data Management "safety net."

Different parts of your Data Management/Data Governance (DM/DG) organization will often require distinct approaches to support the various needs of the Business. In order to ensure "Data Governance interoperability" (i.e., to ensure that everybody plays nicely together), we need to define consistent goals, approaches, and controls. We do this not to tie people's hands, but (returning to our mountain road analogy) to ensure that they don't drive off the cliff when somebody comes unexpectedly around a blind curve. Both on the road and in our Data Governance efforts, we need to communicate clearly what is expected of our drivers/practitioners (e.g., the "Blind Curve Ahead" sign is useless if posted past the bend it is warning us about). Far from limiting what people can do, this clear communication grants a degree of freedom. Many mountain roads have periodic areas where we expect slow-moving vehicles to pull off the road for a few moments to allow more confident drivers to proceed closer to the speed limit. Similarly, well-thought-out DM/DG guardrails create an environment where cutting-edge approaches can co-exist with more basic approaches while still operating as a coherent whole.

To control things at scale, you need a high degree of consistency, and that means not only having Guardrail documents throughout your organization but guardrails that work together as a coherent whole, each reinforcing the intent and meaning of the others in a manner that creates a secure edifice to create an integrated hierarchy of guardrails that provides clear guidance at every turn.

In my many years as an advisory consultant, as well as in my former role as Senior Vice President at a large, multi-national bank, I have seen and heard far too many tales of Data Governance initiatives staffed with people who are reluctant to talk to one another, recalcitrant in sharing ideas and, in short, far too willing to stifle worthy efforts with "not invented here" or "that's not the way WE do it" concerns. If you've moved beyond that in your organization, CONGRATULATIONS! You're part of the leading-edge minority. But even if you've got a culture that respects the notion of a common set of guiding principles, are you defining those principles in a manner that maximizes the commonality of approach (for economies of scale) while respecting the need for different parts of your organization to operate in a way that is optimal to their specific requirements?

Holistic Data Governance Explanation

What most companies, large and small, regardless of business sector, need to establish is a sense of **Holistic Data Governance**. What is Holistic Data Governance?

> *Data Governance that is aware of both the needs of the organization as a whole and as the sum of its parts, and that establishes firm guardrails to ensure consistency across the whole company.*

In this book, we'll examine a *hierarchy* of data governance guardrails where every type of guardrail exists not only to guide (or constrain) what the organization can and cannot do but also to reinforce the establishment, enforcement and outcome of all the other guardrails. In short, I intend to define a *Holistic* approach to Data Governance that establishes consistent mandates from the most generalized corporate vision through all policies and procedures, right on down to specific implementation project plans.

There is a kind of "Cascading Logic" in this approach. Namely:

> ➤ Companies need to control their data to ensure that it supports the needs of their business.

> ➤ In order to do this, we need documented controls in the areas of:
>   • Strategy
>   • Governance
>   • Execution.

> ➤ Each of these levels requires a number of specifically focused guardrails.

The primary focus of this book will be on the hierarchy of documents that will address each of these levels in a consistent and readily manageable way.

One

Finding Common Ground

B efore discussing a *Holistic Hierarchy of Data Governance Guardrails*, let's review some basic terminology. If you're reading a book like this, the terminology and concepts are unlikely to be new. Perhaps you have specific thoughts about one or more parts of this hierarchy. But, just as I am proposing a hierarchy that espouses clear understanding across an entire organization, I'd like to ensure that we have a common ground of understanding about what I mean when I use some of these seemingly "obvious" terms. If you have slightly different notions about some of these distinctions, that shouldn't get in the way of your finding value in the book, but I want you to be clear about what *I* mean when I speak about these things.

Data Management vs Data Governance

First, let's talk about Data Management and Data Governance. The fine points of difference are not especially relevant to the topics covered in this book, but I think it's worth starting with some high-level definitions.

I will use the term Data Management to refer to the resources (human, technological, and financial) that enable or perform the tasks involved in defining and maintaining data and in moving that data around the organization. These activities may or may not exist within an integrated and formalized Data Management Program or Function in your organization, but I will collectively refer to this group as the Data Management Function or the Data Management Initiative.

Data Governance will refer to the resources (again, human, technological, or financial) that *ensure* that the data (and its movement) are performed in accordance with a set of *guardrail documents* (Policies, Standards, Processes, etc.). In most organizations, the Data Governance Function is also the group tasked with creating and maintaining those guardrail documents. However, that may vary in your organization. The Data Governance Function will most likely be a fairly integrated group, It may exist only at the corporate (or "enterprise") level but it might also encompass (additionally or alternately) a group of Operating Unit-specific oversight boards working with varying degrees of coordination. For the purposes of this book, I will assume that there is a coherent Data Governance Function, whether containing a single or multiple bodies.

Where the Data Management and/or Data Governance Functions are officially organized into coordinated functions, there are three basic relationships they can have with one another:

A. Data Governance can be a higher-level function that oversees what Data Management does (see Figure 3.A).

B. Data Governance can be at the same hierarchical level as Data Management while still having an independent oversight role (see Figure 3.B).

C. Data Governance and Data Management can be part of the same organization while, once again, still having oversight and a degree of enforcement authority over the actions of Data Management (see Figure 3.C).

Regardless of which of these corresponds to your organization,[1] the arrangement will have minimal impact on our discussions, but I will call out the distinctions when necessary. In particular, I will frequently need to refer to the combination of the Data Management *and* Data Governance Functions with the phrase, "Data Management/Data Governance Initiative" (often abbreviated as DM/DG). Such terminology is not meant to imply that I'm referring to DM and DG as part of the same

---

[1] If *none* of these seems to describe your structure, you probably have something that is a hybrid of two or more of these approaches. If you have a mature Data Management/Data Governance initiative and you are structured in a completely different manner than any of these options, please email me (my contact information is in the Author's Biography at the end of this book).

function, but only that the topic applies equally to Data
Management *and* Data Governance.

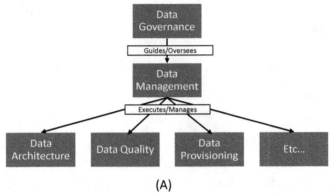

(A)

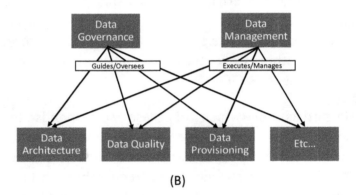

(B)

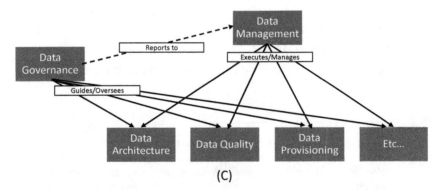

(C)

Figure 3: How Data Governance can relate to Data Management

Options: Decentralized, Centralized, or Federated

Another set of structural terms refers to the overall organization of your organization. First is the question of where Data Governance and Data Management happen. Again, we have three possible configurations:

In a *Decentralized* arrangement, there is 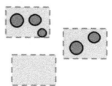 little or no coordination of concepts or standards around the organization. Different parts of the organization define and execute concepts or standards independently. This creates a risk of both redundancy and incompatibility, with the associated inefficiency of frequently having the same problem solved repeatedly by these different operating units. This occasionally works well, but that's mostly in organizations that, by the nature of their business, have many independent subsidiaries.

 The other extreme, not surprisingly, is what we call a *Centralized* approach. Here, everything is defined and often executed by a central authority. This provides economies of scale and ensures consistent control over execution. You don't continually reinvent the wheel, but you may very well constrain the ability of individual Operating Units to perform tasks that are specifically related to their part of the business, forcing them, in effect, to revert to a Decentralized approach for such business-specific needs. This can be effective in environments where most of the Data Management and Data Governance needs can be implemented, for example, in a central repository such as a Data Warehouse or Data Lake.

Finally, we have the **Federated** approach, in which the concepts and standards are *defined* centrally but *implemented* locally. This offers a high degree of central control while allowing for Operating Unit-specific needs. This is the most flexible of the three arrangements since it provides a consistent set of guardrails while allowing the individual Operating Units to implement solutions according to their needs, *provided that they comply with the centrally defined guardrails.*

In practice, most companies employ a hybrid of these three, the most common being a fundamentally Federated approach but with widely shared data managed in a central repository. Much of what we discuss in this book will be most relevant to a Federated approach, yet some concepts may apply to a Centralized or Decentralized approach. Unless otherwise stated, we will always assume a Federated approach by default.

Multi-layered Organizations

A final set of distinctions concerns the different parts of the organization. Consider the excerpt of an organizational structure shown in Figure 4.

The **Enterprise** or **Corporate** level is the top-level controlling entity. It is where your Data Management and

Data Governance Executives sit. In a Federated model, it is where the majority of the Guardrail Documents originate.

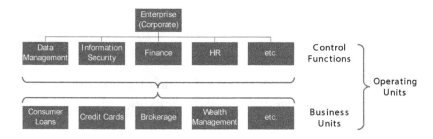

Figure 4: Operating levels

Control Functions are those parts of the organization that provide some kind of service to all the various Business Units (in fact, some organizations refer to these as "Shared Services" rather than "Control Functions"). As we will see, Data Management (and Data Governance) is a Control Function but many of the other Control Functions will also have something to say about what is done with data. Information Security and Privacy are very obvious instances, but Finance and Legal may also have policies that impact how to manage data, and so may HR.

Business Units (or ***Lines of Business***) are the customer-facing parts of the business—the different parts of the organization that offer distinct types of services to those customers. Figure 4 shows some typical Business Units for a Bank, but the distinction is equally applicable regardless of your industry.

Operating Units is a term I'll use to refer collectively to Control Functions *and* Business Units. Put more simply, we refer to Enterprise activities as the centralized, "top of house" activities and Operating-Unit activities as the local activities that are either unique to, or have specialized modifications for, distinct parts of the organization.

Data as an Asset

Finally, I'd like to address briefly the often-mentioned but equally often-misunderstood designation of *Data as an Asset*.

The notion of Data as an Asset is almost a cliché by now, but the concept can impact how we manage our data. To be clear, when I refer to a **data asset**, I mean any collection of data owned by an organization that can impact that organization's bottom line. Whether or not such value is *intrinsic* to the data itself (e.g., data that you routinely sell to others) or whether that value is an outcome of how we *manage* the data will vary from situation to situation. It is certainly the case that appropriate management can help us *realize* value from the data, but we must understand its source.

The key point here is that, in order to get value from our data, we need to manage it consistently across the organization—to take a data-centric rather than an application-centric approach. Over the past several years, the notion that data is valuable has increased, but the approach to generating returns from that data has not. All too often, we continue to develop our data in the context of specific business processes or applications, but we fail to see that **value** arises from the ability to collect and correlate information from diverse sources. We need to see data as more than a by-product of day-to-day operations. Enabling data as an asset requires a shift in both mindset and approach. Synthesizing our data into a value-generating whole requires a wide range of sources, but all those sources must be successfully integrated into a coherent whole to realize the synergistic value.

> *We must shift from seeing Data Management as a technology concern and fully embrace it as a business concern.*

The key to creating and maintaining that coherent whole lies in having a *coherent approach* to managing the data. As we stated in the previous chapter, one of the ways to ensure such a coherent approach is to create an integrated set of Data Governance Guardrails that build on the organization's Business Objectives. We want to develop these within the context of a *Strategic* approach to Data Management with Data Governance ensuring that the *Tactical* steps taken to implement that Strategy are meaningful across the organization and are expressed in a coherent manner across the body of Guardrails. In short, we need a ***Holistic Data Governance Guardrail Hierarchy.***

Two

The Guardrail Hierarchy

The notion of a comprehensive set of guardrail documents will not be new to anyone with experience in Data Governance (either as a practitioner or a "practitionee!"). What I expect **will** be new to many is the notion of what I call a Holistic Hierarchy of Guardrail Documents or, simply, The Guardrail Hierarchy. By defining such a hierarchy of documents, we establish what document types we will use to control our Data Management operation. But by defining **relationships** across those documents, we create a "connective tissue" that knits those documents into a coherent whole. This gets to the core notion of what makes the hierarchy "holistic."

In the previous chapter, we described complex organizations using a simple, three-layer hierarchy:

- An Executive Layer.

- A Layer of Control Functions that address different types of governance.

- A Layer of Lines of Business or Functions that execute on the top layer's vision.

What decisions do we make at these three levels? What must be defined? What instructions must flow down through the layers of the organization? We can categorize these instructions into three categories:

- Strategic (related to long-term planning)

- Governance (related to specifications and oversight)

- Execution (related to implementation)

Figure 5 summarizes the needs of each of these categories, showing each as a combination of "W functions" (Where/Why/What/etc.).

Figure 5: What the Guardrail Hierarchy must define

How do these decisions and directions translate into documents in the Guardrail Hierarchy?

Strategically, we want to know *where* we will head, *why* we care, *what* we want to accomplish, and *how* we'll get there. In the **Governance** space, we want to know *what* will ensure that we accomplish our strategic goals. And finally, in the **Execution** space, we want to know *how* we will act to produce the desired results in a timely manner (*when)* (see Figure 6).

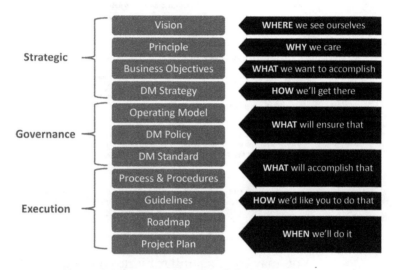

Figure 6: Summary of Guardrail document types

So, where does this get us in our hierarchical thinking?

- We've established that we can think of an organization as having three layers.

- We've identified the types of decisions each layer needs to make.

- We've given names to the types of documents that provide answers to those questions, along with instructions in increasing levels of detail.

So, if these are the areas we want to address, we now must determine the specific types of guardrail documents needed within each level of this hierarchy. The bulk of this book will consist of deep examinations of each of these document types, but Figure 7 provides a high-level overview of them.

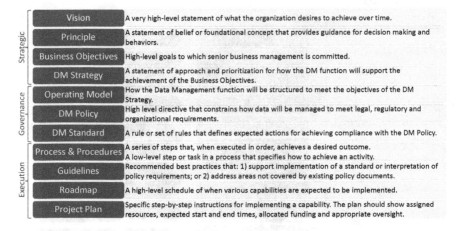

Figure 7: The Holistic Data Governance Guardrail Hierarchy

 You may have a similar hierarchy of documents in place in your organization. Some terms I've heard to describe such a hierarchy include "Universal Requirements," "Policy Hierarchy," "Guideline Hierarchy," or simply "Document Hierarchy." These hierarchies may or may not include everything (or anything!) that I've shown in Figure 7, and maybe such an alternative structure serves your DM/DG environment well. Since I'm writing a book about it, it should be obvious that I recommend the above structure, but even if you choose to deviate from these particular document types, the most important thing is that you think of them holistically as an integrated hierarchy. Ask yourself:

- Have I addressed all requisite levels of specificity?

- How do the documents relate to one another?

- How do they relate to other data-related mandates in the organization?

- How do they support one another?

---

*In my experience, many organizations have given little or no thought to how the documents in the middle of this hierarchy (the **Governance** layer) relate to one another. The documents at the top (the **Strategic** layer) are often ignored altogether and those at the bottom (the **Execution** layer) are rarely considered to be of any interest to the Data Governance function.*

Nevertheless, this specific hierarchy is applicable whether your organization is a couple of hundred people or a couple of hundred thousand people—whether you're in Retail, Research, Pharmaceuticals, or Finance. In any of these environments, this conceptual hierarchy can provide a *concise* and *holistic* approach to addressing the areas we need to control.

As we move down the hierarchy, we progress from high-level directional documents through specific planning and governance documents to detailed execution documents. We will examine each of these in detail as we move through this book, but Figure 8 summarizes some of the principal characteristics of each type.

Strategic

Vision
Aspirational; General; Not Enforceable

Principle
Foundational; High-level; Not Enforceable

Business Objectives
Directional, Specific goals, set by Executive Management (the Business), not by Data Management

DM Strategy
Directional; Aligned to Business Objectives; Accountability lies with leadership

Governance

Operating Model
Structural approach, Prescriptive but at an organizational (rather than activity) level

DM Policy
High-level but enforceable and auditable. Mandatory compliance.

DM Standard
Specific, enforceable and auditable. Infrastructure independent. Mandatory compliance.

Execution

Process & Procedures
Highly specific, enforceable and auditable. Infrastructure specific. Mandatory compliance.

Guidelines
General in nature but may be specific to one or more activities. Recommended but not required. Not enforceable.

Roadmap
Planning document. "30,000 foot view." Dates may be approximate. Subject to change and regular review.

Project Plan
Initiative-specific; Managed Execution. Contingencies may be built in but timing should be respected.

Figure 8: Characteristics of each Guardrail document type

The key is not to have a **lot** of documents (indeed, as we'll see, I recommend only a single instance of several of these document types). What *is* critical is to have a lot of *relationships* between and among the documents. I refer to these relationships as the "Connective Tissue" which knits the various pieces of the hierarchy into a coherent whole. We will reveal the individual threads of this Connective Tissue as we discuss each of the individual guardrail types over the following chapters. A diagram depicting all of the Connective Tissue is shown in Appendix B.

THREE

The Guardrail Document Types

Over the next several chapters, we will explore each document type listed in our Guardrail Hierarchy. We will begin by examining what I call the "Common Matter." This collection of short sections should be included in most (if not necessarily all) of the document types to provide everything from context to basic versioning information.

From there, we will devote a separate chapter to each Guardrail Document type. Although the level of detail in each of these chapters will vary with the complexity of the specific document type, each chapter will provide:

- An overview of the document type.

- The role(s) or group(s) we would expect to create and manage the document.

- Some discussion of the appropriate level of specificity of language in the document.

- Why this document type matters—both within the overall structure of the hierarchy and to the governance of our Data and our Data Management Program.

- Some representative sample language.

- Whether or not all Common Matter sections are relevant for this particular document type.

Additionally, for the more complex document types, I'll provide a detailed breakdown of the sections I recommend as comprising that specific document type.

And because some people may find it surprising to see some of these document types included in the Guardrail Hierarchy, I'll also discuss whether or not each type is "really" a Data Governance Guardrail document (and, if it isn't, why it belongs in the hierarchy anyway!).

Finally, as we will see repeatedly, what makes this Guardrail Hierarchy a *Holistic* Guardrail Hierarchy is the notion of the Connective Tissue we mentioned in the previous chapter. In each chapter from the **Principles** on down, we'll look at how the document type under discussion incorporates an extension of or a response to something defined elsewhere in the hierarchy. Usually, those "somethings" will come from the document type one layer higher in the hierarchy, but occasionally, influences will be woven across more "distant" parts of the structure. Far from being less relevant, these more distant relationships evince the multi-faceted connections that make the hierarchy not merely linked, but truly integrated.

FOUR

Common Matter

As we mentioned in the Introduction, this is a book about *publishing* your guardrail hierarchy. The publishing world uses the term "Common Matter" to refer to material shared across multiple documents. There is Common Matter across most document types in the Holistic Data Governance Guardrail Hierarchy as well. The intent of this Common Matter is to make the documents more readily "consumable" (i.e., meaningful to the widest possible audience) by presenting, in a consistent manner, certain context-providing and "bookkeeping" information for each document. In some cases, we can include this information by referring to a master reference document, but, in general, each specific document should contain the following sections. Each section can appear either as a preamble (i.e., at the front of the document) or as one or more appendices. I have seen both approaches used by different companies, and it's really just a question of what your corporate communications style standards have to say about the matter. The most important concern is simply that the information appears *somewhere* in the document.

 It is unlikely (although certainly possible) that some of these sections would be *prohibited* by your various usage standards, so you may have to make minor adjustments to what I recommend. You may also have additional sections beyond these that are *required* by your internal publishing protocols. Understand your organization's mandates and adjust accordingly.

Rationale

This section is intended to answer the fundamental question, "WHY does this specific document matter to *our* organization?" It provides the underlying reasons and justifications for establishing the document, highlighting its significance to the organization, its intended audience, and how it relates to the other governance guardrails.

Do not generalize here. Although different documents may have similar rationales (especially across different instances of a single document type, such as various Data Management Standards), you want to provide language that is meaningful to the specific document you are introducing. Be concise here, but say enough to clarify why compliance with the current document is important to achieving the organization's Business Objectives. For example: "This strategy lays out the high-level strategic goals and activities by which we will manage and govern our data in order to deliver maximal support in achieving the Organization's Business Objectives."

Scope and Applicability

This section specifies the data that is covered by the particular guardrail (since few documents relate to **all** data[2]) and, if relevant, **who** must comply with the mandates in the document. Additionally, you may have scoping language to address the document's relevance to different geographic regions or specific Operating Units or Roles. Broadly applicable guardrails, such as the Data Management Policy, may refer to the data that is designated as strategically important by the Data Strategy (see Chapter 9). For example: "This policy applies to all data which the Data Strategy identifies as being in-scope." More focused guardrails may provide specific scoping such as "This process must be followed whenever exporting data that includes Personally Identifiable Information (PII)."

In addition to specifying the scope of data to which the guardrail applies, you'll also specify *who* must comply. Although some guardrails may be written to apply to a select subset of the overall organization, most of them will contain general language like "All employees, contractors, and third parties who perform any of the activities identified above must comply with this [policy/standard/etc.]." Do not make the mistake of specifying applicability *only* when it is focused. Although the normative applicability may be "everyone," it is worth

---

[2] In fact, I always treat it as a red flag when I see anything scoped to apply to "all data" in a guardrail. A literal interpretation of such a phrase makes enforcement highly impractical if not outright impossible. You can't "boil the ocean" and *some* kind of scoping is always advisable.

specifying that in each and every guardrail document that contains one or more mandates.[3]

Compliance

The Compliance section outlines expectations for demonstrating adherence to the guardrail's mandates, mechanisms for overseeing such adherence, and processes for managing exceptions and escalations. The first two of those are usually brief specifications. For example:

> *The Data Steward for each Business Unit is responsible for ensuring that practitioners in his/her Business Unit comply with this document. Such compliance is further subject to periodic review by Internal Audit.*

This section also provides information about how to request or escalate exception requests and other non-compliance-related concerns. These processes are not intended to be defined within the Common Matter. Rather, we expect that the processes are defined elsewhere and that we will reference those definitions from within the Common Matter. For example, "Requests for exceptions to the mandates described in this document should be made in accordance with the *Corporate Compliance Exception Request Process*." Any such referenced process should also

---

[3] As we will see when we begin our deep examinations of the individual guardrail types (starting in Chapter 6), some of the guardrails in our hierarchy are intended to provide advice or guidance and, as such, are insufficiently specific to require true compliance.

be listed in the "Related Control Function Documents" section of the Common Matter (q.v., below). [4]

Finally, some organizations may wish to call out the penalties for not complying with specific guardrails. This may be a blanket statement ("Prolonged non-compliance with this Policy will be considered grounds for dismissal.") or may be more qualified:

> *All employees, contractors, and partners must comply with this policy. Compliance will be evidenced through regular reviews by the Data Governance Compliance Group. Any requests for delayed compliance will be treated as performance deficiencies and will be permitted only in exceptional cases. The Data Governance Committee must approve any such delays.*

Related Control Function Documents

Even a fully Holistic Data Governance Guardrail Hierarchy does not exist in a vacuum. There are typically many

---

[4] It varies from organization to organization, but it's unusual for an organization to grant long-term or blanket compliance exceptions (this is especially true in the case of Policies). While short-term exceptions may be necessary in some cases, it is recommended that these be granted for a defined, limited period and that there be some kind of "data debt" (equivalent to the "technical debt" incurred by development teams when they fail to comply with all standards) to incent the groups incurring the "debt" to remediate their non-compliance in a timely manner.

Control Functions[5] throughout the organization that will have things to say about how data is utilized. Most commonly, this will include Information Security and Privacy, but may also include groups like Data Ethics, Regulatory Compliance, and Cross Border Data Movement if these are relevant to your organization. These Control Functions will have policies and/or standards that must be considered, and such documents should be called out in this section of the Common Matter if they potentially interact with the current Data Governance Guardrail.

You may also want to use this section to refer to processes relevant to the current guardrail, such as a Compliance Exception Request process. It is useful to provide a concise list of policies, standards, or procedures that intersect with or enhance the effectiveness of the current document. You may also reference anything that demonstrates integration and alignment with broader organizational controls. Ideally, there will be no conflicts between these other guardrails and the current document, but you may find it useful to state which documents will take precedence if such conflicts do occur (for example, see Figure 9).

---

[5] We discussed Control Functions in Chapter 1 but, as a reminder, we use the term Control Function to refer to any oversight or "shared service" function within the company. Common examples are Information Security, Privacy, Human Resources, Finance, etc.). While we will occasionally need to refer to these Control Functions distinct from Business Units within the organization, we will more commonly use the term "Operating Unit" to refer to any Control Function *or* Business Unit.

> **Related Control Function Documents**
> 1. Information Security Proper Handling of Secure Data (Policy IS103)
> 2. Corporate Data Privacy Policy (Policy DP101)
> 3. Required Metadata Attributes Standard (Standard DM207)
> 4. Vendor Management Policy & Procedures (Policy VM103)
> 5. Guidelines for Effective Data Controls (Guidelines DC101)
>
> NOTE: All related documents can be found by clicking on the hyperlinks above or by connecting to the Enterprise Guardrails Portal at https://EGP.com. If you are outside the company's firewall, standard login procedures must be followed.

Figure 9: Related Control Function Documents example

Accountability

This section is typically very brief and identifies the role or body that is accountable for the current content of the document and that is responsible for ensuring that it is updated as needed (or as required by periodic review mandates). This section should never identify specific individuals but, rather, specify roles that will resolve to one or more individuals at any given point in time (e.g., say "the [current] Chief Data Officer" rather than "John Smith"). This nuance will minimize the need to update the document in response to role changes. In addition to identifying the owner of the document or document section, you may also wish to call out the primary responsibilities associated with that ownership. For example: "The CDO owns this strategy and is responsible for its maintenance, updates, and adherence to regulatory requirements."

Publish and Approval Log

This is a simple table listing the version history, publication dates, and approvals related to the document. This provides a clear historical record of changes and endorsements, fostering transparency and accountability and serving as an aid in auditing or adjudicating compliance issues. For example:

Publication & Approval Log for DM101
Enterprise Data Management Policy

Version	Action	Actor	Date	Comments
1.0	Submit for Review	EDM Policy Working Group	Jan 7, 2020	Completed Working Draft submitted for DG Council review
1.0	Review	DG Council	Jan 15, 2020	Approved as is
1.0	Approve	CDO	Jan 22, 2020	Approved as is
1.0	Publish	Guardrail Custodian	Jan 23, 2020	Posted to Guardrail Portal
1.1	Submit for Review	EDM Policy Working Group	May 1, 2021	Address changes mandated by CPRA
1.1	Review	DG Council, Compliance, Legal	June 1, 2021	Approved as is
1.1	Reject	CDO	June 8, 2021	CPRA section 1798.105 not adequately addressed
1.1	Submit for Review	EDM Policy Working Group	Jun 22, 2021	Further updates to address 1789.105
1.1	Review	DG Council, Compliance, Legal	June 30, 2021	Approved as is
1.1	Approve	CDO	July 2, 2021	Approved as is
1.1	Publish	Guardrail Custodian	July 3, 2021	Current Version

Figure 10: Publish and Approval Log example

Glossary

I highly recommend that all guardrail documents minimize jargon and acronyms. Even when such terms seem very clear to the author(s), different parts of the organization may use those terms differently. Even if certain terms and acronyms are in common usage around the organization, they can easily present stumbling blocks to new hires, contractors, and other temporary workers or third parties. Outside regulators (if these are relevant to your industry) may also be unfamiliar with such language.

> ### *What's THAT mean?*
>
> In the banking industry, the commonly used term "REPO" indicates the re-possession of collateral to someone in the collateralized loans group but the exact same term would indicate a Repurchase Agreement to someone in the Deposits group. These meanings are so "obvious" to each group that a conversation across the two groups may have to go very far "off the rails" before one or both groups realize that they have different definitions of the term.

Despite all best intentions to refrain from such terminological shortcuts, a total avoidance of them can result in awkward language that hampers the readability of a document. It is, therefore, imperative to include a Glossary *in each document* so that new readers are clear about what they're reading. This Glossary should define any acronyms, technical terms, or potentially ambiguous terms used in the document.

Please note that we follow our own advice and have a Glossary at the end of this book!

FIVE

Strategic Guardrails

Our guardrail documents group into three broad categories: Strategic, Governance, and Execution. In the next four chapters, we will delve into the four types of documents that collectively define our foundational strategy for how we will approach the Governance and Management of our Data.

- We will examine a high-level *Vision* statement defining where we are and where we see ourselves headed.

- We will develop broad *Guiding Principles* that will define why we care about certain things and provide slightly more specific guidance on how we will operate within Data Governance and Data Management.

- We will incorporate the *Business Objectives* defined by our executive management, focusing on those objectives that will directly impact how we manage and govern our data.

- Finally, in the most lengthy chapter in this section, we will examine the ***Data and Data Management Strategy***, in which we define strategic goals and activities, lay out a strategic plan for how we will structure our program, and examine how we will assess our program.

Figure 11: Execution Guardrails

Six

Vision Statement

What the organization desires to achieve over time.

W e've all seen Vision Statements, even if our companies don't have one. These are the aspirational and, ideally, *inspirational* short statements that sum up why we do what we do and where we see ourselves going. We may define these statements at the corporate level, but individual Operating Units may have their own complementary Vision Statements. More relevant to the current discussion, the Data Management/Data Governance organization should have its own Vision Statement. This may or may not be identical to the Vision Statement of the overall business. Identical or not, we are not looking for any detail here. We are not looking for a full-blown strategy. Instead, we are looking for a statement of how we see DM/DG supporting the business and, optionally, how we see DM/DG evolving over time.

In short, a Vision Statement provides a very high-level view of what's important to DM/DG and what we would like to see DM/DG achieve over time.

The DM/DG Vision Statement should be:

- **Aspirational** – Take what I call the "grounded magic wand" approach when crafting it. In other words, be realistic, but use wording that describes how you see the function operating in a best-case scenario.

- **"For" something** – The Vision Statement should not be pablum aimed at some kind of pie-in-the-sky attempt at inspiration. Tie it to one or two very high-level but meaningful goals, perhaps with hypothetical outcomes: "We will ensure that our data fully supports the achievement of the company's business objectives and delight our customers with the sense that we understand and respect their needs."

- **Inclusive** – Avoid any hints of language that may make any parts of the organization feel excluded. If your Vision Statement celebrates a move to cutting-edge technology, ask yourself how this lands for people working in more conventional Operating Units such as General Ledger.

- **Resilient** – By definition, a Vision Statement should be VISIONARY! You should not have to recraft your Vision every time the market shifts or the company undergoes a routine organizational realignment. Ideally, the same Vision Statement will be equally applicable in good times and bad.

Some overall corporate Vision Statements may also work as a DM/DG Vision statement, perhaps with minor tweaking. For example, "We will be the company with which we, ourselves, would want to do business." In a best-case scenario, however, there will be a DM/DG Vision that is not simply *aligned* with the Corporate Vision Statement but is a direct support for it. If your Corporate Vision Statement says something like:

> *Our number one goal is the complete satisfaction of our customers. We will treat them with respect, always listen to their feedback, and strive to anticipate their needs.*

then an aligned DM/DG Vision Statement might be

> *We will treat each customer's data as we would want our own data to be treated, always understanding that their personal data is **their** data and we are being trusted to manage it with integrity.*

Of course, this is not to say that you should restrict your DM/DG Vision to a single sentence or even a single Vision Statement. Different parts of the organization may have their own Vision Statements, and different parts of the DM/DG organization may have separate Vision Statements. In all cases, an overall summarizing statement makes for an effective rallying cry, but if you need to write a paragraph or even a couple of paragraphs on the topic, feel free to do so. Just keep in mind that this is the top of the hierarchy. You want to speak in broad, sweeping terms here. There will be ample opportunities in subsequent documents to elaborate on why you think something is important, how you'll structure your practice to achieve those things, what associated mandates and processes will be developed around them, and so forth. Julius Caesar may have had a *vision* for what Rome could be, but, as we all know, Rome wasn't built in a day. Keep things simple and aspirational for now. It's also important that if you *do* create multiple Vision Statements, you ensure that they are compatible with one another. You may have a Data Quality Vision that is distinct from your overall Data Management Vision, but you do not want that more focused Data Quality Vision Statement to contradict the broader DM/DG Vision Statement.

Such a high-level statement is not necessarily a Guardrail of and in itself. We include it in our Guardrail Hierarchy because it *guides* what should be mandated by the more formal Guardrails. It anchors all the other documents in a formally espoused "ground of being." The Vision Statement says "who we are" in the matter of DM/DG. It will immediately provide context for our Statement of Principles (see Chapter 7), yet it will also help anchor (directly or indirectly) all the other Guardrails in our Hierarchy. Although senior DM/DG management will normally write the DM/DG Vision Statement, input should be solicited from a wide range of stakeholder groups to ensure it speaks broadly across the organization.

Despite the attention we paid to Common Matter in the previous chapter, some may consider it overly formal to incorporate all of our Common Matter sections into the Vision Statement document. Most specifically, because a Vision Statement *guides* rather than *mandates*, the sections on Scope and Compliance are explicitly irrelevant to our documented Vision (and the language of our Vision should **definitely** not give rise to the need for its own Glossary!).

The other Common Matter sections are all worth considering for inclusion, however.

Category	Strategic
Name	Vision
Description	A very high-level statement of what the organization desires to achieve over time.
What	**WHERE** WE SEE OURSELVES
Sample Level of Specificity	"We are a community of data literate information champions."
Characteristics	Aspirational; General; Not Enforceable.

Table 1: Characteristics of Vision Statement

Principles

A Vision Statement grounds us in a general way of thinking about how we operate. At the next level of the hierarchy, we need to begin to articulate some basic principles that guide how we will operate. From a DM/DG perspective, this encapsulates those beliefs or foundational concepts that most succinctly identify how we want to manage and govern our data. Put a bit more prosaically, the Principles define what *kinds* of approaches we will take to demonstrate why we care about what we do, and that will guide decision-making and behaviors.

As with the Vision Statement, concise but clear language is the rule here. Remember that these are not mandates. Rather, they provide general guidance for situations in which the most appropriate application of the formal mandates may be ambiguous or for situations where we have failed to create any formal mandates.

There are many types of principles:

- Operating principles
- Ethical principles
- Behavioral principles
- Guiding principles.

Each of these has a place in the overall operation of the organization as well as within DM/DG. We will focus on Guiding Principles for our Guardrail Hierarchy, but most of what we say about these will also apply to other types of Principles.

Guiding Principles are a set of broadly stated "rules of thumb" that further ground us (beyond the Vision Statement) and which "set the tone" for how we will operate. Although more specific than the Vision Statement, these are still not mandates, and precisely detailed language is neither necessary nor appropriate.

Since Principles may originate from business, legal, or regulatory sources, it is typically our DM/DG executives, often in conjunction with business executives, who will develop them. Once again, solicit input from all stakeholder groups to help ensure relevance across the organization. We saw that, with the Vision Statement, there is often a very close relationship between the wording of the Corporate Vision Statement and the DM/DG Vision Statement. However, where our Corporate Guiding Principles may bear on how we operate within DM/DG (we are, after all, part of the larger corporate structure), the

DM/DG Guiding Principles may be more subtly linked to the Corporate Principles and will, of course, be more directly related to data or data management. For example, where the Corporate Principles may include something like "We will treat all our employees as being critical to our success as a company," our DM/DG Principles will typically be more along the lines of "We will always use our customers' data as we would like **our** data to be used."

Although our Principles are high-level and concise, we will see over the next several chapters that they provide points of alignment to numerous other locations within our **Holistic Data Governance** Guardrail Hierarchy. Some of our Principles will relate more directly to overall business goals and will find themselves informing our Business Objectives (see Chapter 8), while others will be more immediately relevant to achieving our Data Management Strategic Goals and Activities (see Chapter 9). Additionally, the Principles will be among our considerations when developing our Data Management Policy mandates (see Chapter 12).

Similar to Vision Statements, a high-level Statement of Principles is not necessarily a Guardrail of and in itself. The reason for including Principles in our Guardrail Hierarchy is, once again, that they guide what should be mandated by the more formal Guardrails. They anchor all the other documents in articulating those concepts that we consider relevant to what we do. The Statement of Principles defines how we will operate within DM/DG. Although senior DM/DG management will normally write the DM/DG Principles, we should solicit input from all stakeholder groups to ensure that it speaks to a broad range of these stakeholders.

Despite the attention we paid to Common Matter in Chapter 4, some may consider it overly formal to incorporate all of our Common Matter sections into the Principles document. Most specifically, because Principles are guidance rather than compulsory mandates, the sections on Scope and Compliance are explicitly irrelevant to our documented Principles (and the language of our Principles should **definitely** not give rise to the need for its own Glossary!). The other Common Matter sections are all worth considering for inclusion, however.

In this section, we have focused on Guiding Principles, but some organizations may also wish to formulate Operating, Ethical, or Behavioral Principles. Bear in mind, though, that there are often other Control Functions providing guidance in those areas and it may be more appropriate for them to author such Principles.

Category	Strategic
Name	Principle
Description	A statement of belief or foundational concept that guides decision-making and behaviors.
What	**WHY** WE CARE
Sample Level of Specificity	"We will always operate in accordance with our code of data ethics."
Characteristics	Foundational; High-level; Not Enforceable.

Table 2: Characteristics of Principle

EIGHT

Business Objectives

High-level goals to which senior management is committed.

The primary goal of the DM/DG function is to ensure that the business has ready access to the data that it needs to operate and that the users trust this data.[6] To ensure that the data supports the business in achieving their objectives, it is critical that these objectives be clearly documented and shared with the DM/DG function.

These high-level Business Objectives are developed by Executive Management and define results and targets that business planners or executives intend to achieve within a

---

[6] The DM/DG function also plays an important role, usually in conjunction with the Information Security and Privacy functions (and, perhaps, the Compliance function) in ensuring that sensitive data of any sort (PI/PII or otherwise) is secured against unauthorized access and use.

stated time. We can define Business Objectives at the level of the Enterprise or Business Unit. At both levels, the authors will have many short-, mid-, and long-term business goals for the organization. Data Management must determine how to manage the data in ways that best support achieving these objectives. While we should document all the objectives for reference, I recommend that DM/DG *focus* on mid-term and long-term goals, especially those at a high level. It's not that DM doesn't care about the business's achievement of short-term goals. It's just that, for the most part, the short-term goals will connect with very specific initiatives and there won't be time for DM to implement any kind of strategic approach to support their achievement.

Strictly speaking, the list of Business Objectives is **not** a Data Governance guardrail document. The list is not even prepared by the DM/DG team (although DM/DG may provide input). I have included Business Objectives in our Guardrail Hierarchy because, like the Vision Statement and the Principles, they provide critical grounding for how DM/DG will operate. As we will see in the next chapter, the primary point where these Objectives will be "injected" into the hierarchy will be via the Data Management Strategy. Still, having the Business Objectives documented as a distinct "quasi-guardrail" is useful in stressing their importance in shaping the overall formulation and prioritization of what DM/DG will do. We will see as we move through the levels of our Guardrail Hierarchy that these Business Objectives will serve as fundamental guidance for crafting the more formal guardrail documents. From the Data Management Strategy down, the guardrails will increasingly be providing explicit statements of how data will be managed and governed to best support the achievement of the Business Objectives.

Although Executive Management typically develops the Business Objectives, it is up to Data Management/Data Governance executives to determine how DM/DG will develop strategic goals and associated activities to support achieving those Objectives. In the next chapter, we'll examine in greater detail how to define such goals and activities within the Data Management Strategy but, to make the **Holistic Data Governance** Guardrail Hierarchy, well, a bit more *Holistic*, it can be valuable to include high-level summaries of these strategic goals and activities in your Objectives document, showing how they relate to the individual Business Objectives. For example, if we have a business goal of:

> *Our goal this year is to improve customer satisfaction by 25%.*

Then some supporting Strategic Goals or Activities could be:

- *Ensure that all data has an approved and enforced "golden source."*
- *Enact new controls to catch inaccurate customer data before it is ingested.*

Alternatively, given a more immediately data-related Business Objective like:

> *We will proactively seek out new market segments in the coming year.*

We can develop associated strategic activities such as:

- *Invest in predictive analytics and AI to facilitate market analysis.*

- *Subscribe to third-party market data to help identify relevant target segments.*

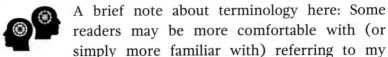 A brief note about terminology here: Some readers may be more comfortable with (or simply more familiar with) referring to my "Strategic Goals" as "Data Objectives" or "Data Management Objectives." I will use the term "Strategic Goals" (along with their associated "Strategic Actions") to emphasize that these are goals (and actions) in *support of* but *distinct from* the Business Objectives established by senior business management.

Despite our attention to Common Matter, some may still consider it overly formal to incorporate all of our "Common Matter" sections into the Business Objectives document. Nonetheless, we are entering a slightly different area of focus than what we discussed with respect to Vision and Principles in the previous two chapters. Although the achievement of such objectives is typically a key factor in assessing the performance of the business leadership, these Business Objectives are (by definition) generally not compulsory for DM/DG—at least not in the same way as compliance with the guardrails that we will examine in the upcoming chapters (Strategy, Policy, Standards, etc.). As we will see in the next chapter, DM/DG executives will have their own set of goals for which they are responsible. These goals will *support* achieving the Business Objectives (as discussed above), but these Data Management Strategic

Goals will involve data-specific activities, and we will assess them using a set of metrics that is distinct from (but that supplement) those used to assess the Business Objectives themselves.

Both the Business Objectives and the next chapter's Strategic Data Management Goals are, strictly speaking, still in the realm of guidance (in the sense of being high-level and directional rather than in the form of specific mandates), and so the sections on Scope and Compliance remain irrelevant at this point in the Hierarchy. Nonetheless, insofar as the Business Objectives drive the Strategic Goals and Actions, achieving those Strategic Goals may factor into the performance reviews of DM/DG executives. As such, we would expect to see a more extensive Rationale section that explicitly lays out the expected role of DM/DG in achieving these Business Objectives.

We have previously said that Vision and Principles statements should be sufficiently clear and simple to require no associated Glossary. However, depending on the nature of your company's business, the Business Objectives could become fairly technical, and so a Glossary may be deemed prudent. As always, the other Common Matter sections are all worth considering for inclusion.

Finally, we will see in the next chapter that the Data Management Strategy is, amongst other things, a key internal marketing document that can be used by DM/DG executives (in particular the CDO[7]) to wave the flag for DM/DG and to garner support from key stakeholders throughout the organization. As such, it may be useful to have a concise "back-pocket" document that lays out the Business Objectives (as described in this chapter) but that also shows how Strategic Data Management Goals will support these Business Objectives (as discussed in the next chapter). Additionally, by adding a high-level Vision Statement, you create a valuable tool, a sort of "Business Case Lite," for initiating meaningful conversations with skeptical stakeholders who need to be convinced of the value of a coherent, enterprise-wide Data Management/Data Governance initiative.

Category	Strategic
Name	Business Objectives
Description	High-level goals to which senior management is committed.
What	**WHAT** WE WANT TO ACCOMPLISH
Sample Level of Specificity	· "To increase our customers' trust in us by at least 15% this year." · "To grow sales of <our new product line> by 20% this year."
Characteristics	Directional; Specific goals; Set by Executive Management (the Business), not by Data Management.

Table 3: Characteristics of Business Objectives

---

[7] Throughout this book, we will use the term CDO (Chief Data Officer) to designate the most senior executive tasked with responsibility for the DM/DG initiative(s). Depending on the size and complexity of your organization, this position may be a Chief Governance Officer, a Chief Data and Analytics Officer, some other C-suite role or, in smaller organizations, a lower-level executive.

NINE

Data Management Strategy and Data Strategy

How Data Management will support the achievement of the objectives.

In my years of assessing Data Management practices across multiple industries, I have been continuously surprised at how few Data Management initiatives, even those led by a CDO, have a formal Data Management Strategy. Even those organizations that **do** have such a strategy frequently fail to document it in a meaningful way. Recall our maxim from the Introduction, *"If it's not written down, it doesn't exist!"* To speak to this shortcoming, beginning with this chapter, we will take a much more explicit look at what I consider best practice[8] in defining each type of guardrail document.

A comprehensive Data Management Strategy (DMS) is critical to fully understanding how you want your Data Management/Data Governance initiative to evolve going forward. Most fundamentally, the Strategy defines your desired target state and what you intend to do to get there. As discussed in the previous chapter, the primary purpose of the Data Management Strategy is to define how to manage data in a manner that best supports the achievement of the high-level Business Objectives. While this may imply that the Strategy is of most immediate concern to senior management, all Data Management practitioners should be aware of its contents because even people who are not directly accountable for the success of the Strategy can benefit from the Strategy's value as a guidance document.

Strategy vs. Tactics

To avoid confusion, let's take a moment to define what we mean by a Strategy. We'll start with a dictionary definition. Merriam-Webster defines "strategy" primarily in military terms:

---

[8] These practices are based on my observations over the years as a senior Data Management/Data Governance leader, as a consultant working with senior DM/DG leaders and on countless conversations with members of DAMA and the EDM Council.

1. *the science and art of employing the political, economic, psychological, and military forces of a nation or group of nations to afford the maximum support to adopted policies in peace or war*

2. *the science and art of military command exercised to meet the enemy in combat under advantageous conditions.*[9]

Despite the militaristic bent in those definitions, the relevance to *business strategy* is in the notion of pre-defining the attainment of "advantageous conditions" when we "meet the enemy." Of course, "meeting the enemy," in business terms (and especially in Data Management terms) is (at least usually!) a question of confronting how we will meet our long-term goals. The Strategy focuses on big objectives (refer back to Chapter 8)—"big" in the sense of "long-term." For example, a strategy is typically updated annually and rarely more than quarterly. In short, the strategy gives us a sense of what goals we want to achieve without being distracted by day-to-day minutiae of short-term distractions.

A *Strategic Plan* (or, more simply, a *Strategy*) is, most fundamentally, a list of our high-level *Strategic Goals* along with the associated *Strategic Actions* that we will take to achieve those Goals (discussed in more detail below). As with the Goals, the *Strategic Actions* will be broadly defined activities, more akin to "We will implement an Enterprise Data Catalog" than to spelling out all the individual steps you would need to actually *implement* such a catalog (define requirements, assess what's out there, make a selection,

---

[9] https://www.merriam-webster.com/dictionary/strategy.

purchase it, install it, configure it, train your users, etc.). By extension, a Data Management Strategy is a statement of approach and prioritization for how the Data Management function will support the achievement of the Business Objectives.

These Strategic Goals and Strategic Actions are distinct from a *Tactical Plan,*[10] which would break your Strategic Goals into their various constituent parts and define the short-term actions necessary to achieve those constituent goals.[11]

Throughout this book, we'll use the term "Strategic Goals" to refer, specifically, to these high-level goals as expressed in our Data Management Strategy. Some of our "lower-level" guardrail documents (i.e., those further down the **Holistic Data Governance Guardrail Hierarchy**) will have more immediate targets. Still, the goals and activities associated with those lower-level guardrails will, in some way or another, support attaining the higher-level Strategic Goals. More generally, whenever we speak of the contents of our Data Management Strategy, remember that we *are*, in fact, speaking *strategically.* In other words, the contents of your Data Management Strategy should be high-level goals with associated high-level actions (or even just *types* of actions). The focus will be on the *kinds* of things we want to accomplish and *why* we consider those to be important.

---

[10] It would be convenient if there were a single word that would serve as a synonym for "Tactical Plan" (in the way that "Strategy" stands for "Strategic Plan"), but I'm unaware of any such word!

[11] Although we will not discuss Tactical Plans in any significant detail in this book, we will briefly revisit them in Chapter 16.

The Strategy is typically not subject to mandatory compliance, per se. Indeed, the nature of the Strategy's language is more directional than constraining and, as such, the document is difficult to monitor for statement-by-statement compliance in the way that a policy or standard would be so monitored.[12] However, senior management often *will* be measured on (and, I would assert, **should** be measured on) how well they are achieving the goals of the Strategy. I have, in fact, encountered real-world situations where *achieving* such goals is a major determinant in the bonus portion of these executives' compensation and/or their overall performance reviews.

Maintaining the Strategy

Authorship of the Data Management Strategy falls primarily to the Data Management executive team. They have the experience to craft a strategic approach to managing the organization's data. That much being said, as with all the guardrails we have discussed so far, you should solicit input from all stakeholder groups.

It is also important to note that, as with many of the documents in our Guardrail Hierarchy, the Strategy is a *living document* that needs to be reviewed regularly. Market conditions change, our business objectives evolve, and our priorities get re-shuffled. You want a Strategy that provides *stability* throughout short-term disruptive events by

---

[12] Auditable compliance will be discussed in more detail in Chapter 12.

focusing on long-term goals, but sometimes, the *path* we've laid out becomes increasingly beset with hurdles.

Figure 12: We may be forced to change direction

To return to the "mountain road" analogy I used in the Introduction, if your current route is no longer viable, it is just plain foolishness to "stay the course." Such viability may not always be assessable in the short term. That's one of the reasons why I recommend reviewing your Data Management Strategy on an annual basis rather than, say, a quarterly basis. Nonetheless, some events are so disruptive (think of the 2008 Financial Crisis or the 2020 COVID-19 lockdown) that mid-cycle re-assessment of your strategy could be merited.

When your Business Objectives change, your Data Management Strategic Goals may or may not need to adapt accordingly. You must always consider how you will continue to create, curate, manage, and govern data so that it provides value, supports compliance and privacy, addresses risk, generates actionable insights for leadership, and, in short, supports the achievement of the Business Objectives.

One Strategy or Many?

This *Enterprise* Data Management Strategy should have the force of being **THE** Data Management Strategy. That much being said, various Operating Units may have reason to craft supplemental strategies. This might be due to the specific nature of their part of the business. For example, any part of an organization that deals primarily with large amounts of externally sourced data or that outsources certain processes to third parties will likely have different or more focused Strategic Goals around the management of metadata (not to mention around the access and use of data) than do Operating Units that create all their own data and operate in a more insular fashion.

Any such Operating Unit-specific Strategic Goals must be aligned with the goals defined in the Enterprise Data Management Strategy. Most fundamentally, this means that the Local goals can't be at odds with the Enterprise goals but it also means that they must be *in support of* those Enterprise Goals. This does not mean that the Operating-Unit-specific goals are meant to be tactical goals, but rather that they are *locally strategic* in a way that underpins the achievement of the broader goal. For example, if the Enterprise has a goal to improve Customer Satisfaction, your Sales Group may have a strategic goal around how a new approach to managing their data can support more effective ways to interact with customers when they sell to them and your Customer Support Group may have distinct but compatible data management goals for how *they* interact with customer concerns, questions, and comments. These goals are still strategic to the distinct Operating

Units, but collectively, they are in service of the more broadly defined Enterprise goal.

Alignment is a two-way street, however. If important Strategic Goals are formulated by one or more of the Operating Units (OUs) and these goals have no higher-level counterpart in the Enterprise Data Management Strategy, a dialog is needed to determine if you should declare an additional goal (or goals) at the Enterprise level. For example, if a number of your Operating Units have compatible but different Strategic Goals around how they will manage their metadata, and you have not incorporated this concept into the Enterprise Strategy, you should consider a generalized Enterprise goal encompassing all of those Local goals. Not only does it turn those Operating Unit-specific goals into expressions of a common Enterprise goal, but it also provides a guardrail to ensure that the various Operating Unit goals *are* compatible. In no case should an Operating Unit be allowed to formulate any strategic goals that directly conflict with those of the Enterprise Data Management Strategy, no matter how well-intentioned or "necessary" they may be.

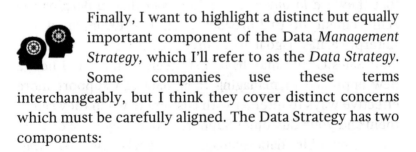

Finally, I want to highlight a distinct but equally important component of the Data *Management Strategy,* which I'll refer to as the *Data Strategy.* Some companies use these terms interchangeably, but I think they cover distinct concerns which must be carefully aligned. The Data Strategy has two components:

- A Data Content Strategy that addresses the identification of the classes or domains of data that are considered most important to attaining the company's Business Objectives and

- A Data Usage Strategy addresses *how* that data will be leveraged to attain those Business Objectives.

I have occasionally seen companies maintain the Data Strategy as a separate document, distinct from the Data Management Strategy, but to emphasize how closely these must be aligned, I will consider Data Content Strategy and Data Usage Strategy to be sub-sections of the Data Management Strategy.

We'll discuss this in more detail in a few pages when we answer the question **What Belongs in a Data Management Strategy?**, but fundamentally, The Data Content Strategy and Data Usage Strategy define (at a high level) the data that is most critical to the achievement of our goals and how we plan to leverage that data to achieve those goals.

Why does this Belong in our Hierarchy?

The Data Management Strategy is the linchpin that links a company's Business Objectives to the day-to-day operations of the Data Management/Data Governance activities. As we'll see below, it translates those Business Objectives into Data Management Goals, which will directly drive everything from Policies and Standards to implementation-specific Project Plans.

Although the Strategy is not enforceable in the same way as Policies and Standards, all those lower-level guardrails are, ultimately, designed to ensure that we achieve the high-level Business Objectives. As such, it is a highly specialized guidance document that informs many (some might say all) of the activities that Data Governance must undertake. It lays out the direction the Data Management team wants to take regarding how to use, manage, and govern data. If it is not the role of Data Governance to *enforce* the Strategy, the Strategy *does* provide prioritization, long-term direction, and a sense of where enforcement is most critical.

Why does this Matter?

The formality of Risk Management varies greatly across industry sectors. Due to the major impact of events like the 9/11 attacks[13] and the 2008 Financial Crisis, the Financial Services sector (and Banking in particular) has been at the forefront of formalized Risk Management. These days, knowledge of a formalized Three Lines of Defense[14] approach to Risk Management is understood even by middle-level management at most medium-to-large-sized banks. In other industries, it may only be various C-suite leaders and their direct reports who truly understand and play significant roles in managing Risk, and their approach may not extend

---

[13] Outside of the Banking world, few people think of the role that the financial industry played in the 9/11 attacks. Theirs's were far from the most egregious failures, but two critical Banking processes (Know Your Customer (KYC) and Anti-money Laundering (AML)) were sufficiently lacking in rigor that multiple bad actors were able to finance the attacks. Regulatory mandates around these processes were strengthened significantly in the aftermath of the attacks.

[14] See the Glossary for a brief discussion of Three Lines of Defense Risk Management.

to a formal Three Levels methodology. Regardless of the formality of Risk Management, Risk impacts all companies. The overall topic of Risk Management is too broad to discuss in any detail in this book, but I do want to say something about the role of our Data Management Strategy in addressing the mitigation of Data Risk.

To be successful, companies need to take risks. Much of this is done intentionally (e.g., trying to break into a new market space is inherently risky, but in any given situation, the potential rewards may be considered to be worth the risk).[15] Unfortunately, companies may inadvertently expose themselves to various types of risk, and Data Risk is a prime example (e.g., allowing broad in-house access to your customer data may simplify many of your processes, but doing so may violate your customers' privacy rights). Much of our Data Risk (which can also impact heavily on Financial, Operational, and Reputational Risk) can be significantly minimized by the relatively simple expedient of garnering executive support for the Data Management initiative. Such top-down understanding of and support for Data Management at this level can translate into an efficient, robust, and sustainable Data Management initiative. Having clearly articulated Business Objectives allows Data Management executives to design Strategic Goals that directly support achieving those Objectives. The greater the degree of such engagement, the stronger our

---

[15] Note that formal Risk Management is far more rigorous than this high-level statement may imply. Risk Management involves quantified assessment of risk exposure, projected returns/rewards, likelihood of realizing those returns/rewards, evaluating all this in light of a predefined "Risk Appetite Statement" and enacting controls that ensure people and systems operate within these established ranges of "acceptable risk."

Data Culture,[16] helping to drive the engagement of all staff in ensuring that Data Management is a sustainable, Business-As-Usual (BAU) endeavor rather than a loosely related string of separate initiatives. This organizational consistency of focus, of getting everyone "rowing in the same direction," leads directly to:

- Efficient detection and resolution of Data and Data Management issues.

- Organization-wide sensitivity to and support for the management of Data Risk.

- Streamlined optimization of business processes.

- Leveraging of the organization's collective knowledge to drive innovation.

These are just some of the ways in which the DMS can have a direct impact on the Return on Investment (ROI) of our Data Management/Data Governance initiative. The actual calculation of such ROI metrics isn't always easy, but easy or not,[17] it should be clear that consistency of focus, cooperative effort, and clearly defined goals can only improve the efficacy of our DM/DG endeavors.

How Much Are You Worth?

Several years ago, I was the senior Enterprise Information Architect at a global bank, and a large part of my job was to develop policies, standards, metrics and the like for our Data Management

---

[16] We'll discuss Data Culture in more detail in Chapter 11.

[17] We'll discuss Metrics in a bit more detail in Chapter 11.

> initiative. I used to say that the value of my group's
> work was that "if you do what we tell you now,
> then you WON'T have such-and-such a problem
> two years from now(!)" That was certainly NOT
> the most lucid statement of value I ever produced,
> but let's face it...measuring the ROI of Data
> Management can be very problematic because it's
> very hard to assign specific cause-and-effect.
> Nevertheless, there are a number of ways in which,
> directly or indirectly, effective DM will have a
> positive impact on your bottom line and it is
> important to develop metrics to demonstrate that
> wherever you can do so convincingly.

What Belongs in a Data Management Strategy?

Whereas some of our Common Matter sections are optional or even irrelevant to some of the higher-level guardrails within the hierarchy, all of the Common Matter sections should be contained within the Data Management Strategy.

Besides such Strategy-specific Common Matter, there are eight main components that I recommend including in your Data Management Strategy. Just as the overall Strategy follows on from the higher level guardrails and forms a basis for the later guardrails in the hierarchy, the eight sections of the DMS work as a multi-faceted statement of the strategic steps we will take to ensure that Data Management is doing all that it can to support the achievement of the overall Business Objectives as defined above. Let's look at these eight sections in more detail.

At this level of the guardrail hierarchy, we still do not concern ourselves with implementation (i.e., *tactical*) details. The point of the Strategy is to provide the strategic underpinnings for accomplishing what we plan to do within our Data Management initiative. You will see repeatedly as we go through these eight sections that there is no effort to describe the *details* of what we will do. Rather, we justify how certain *types* of activity will help us to achieve the Strategic Goals that are spelled out in the first section of the DMS. As we have already pointed out, these Goals, by definition, will support achieving the Business Objectives described in the previous chapter.

Figure 13 provides an overview of the eight recommended components and shows how they group into three main areas:

Program Direction
- Strategic Goals & Actions
- Establishment of Program
- Data Capabilities

Data Strategy
- Data Content
- Data Usage

Program Enablement
- Communications & Training
- Program Metrics
- Data Ethics

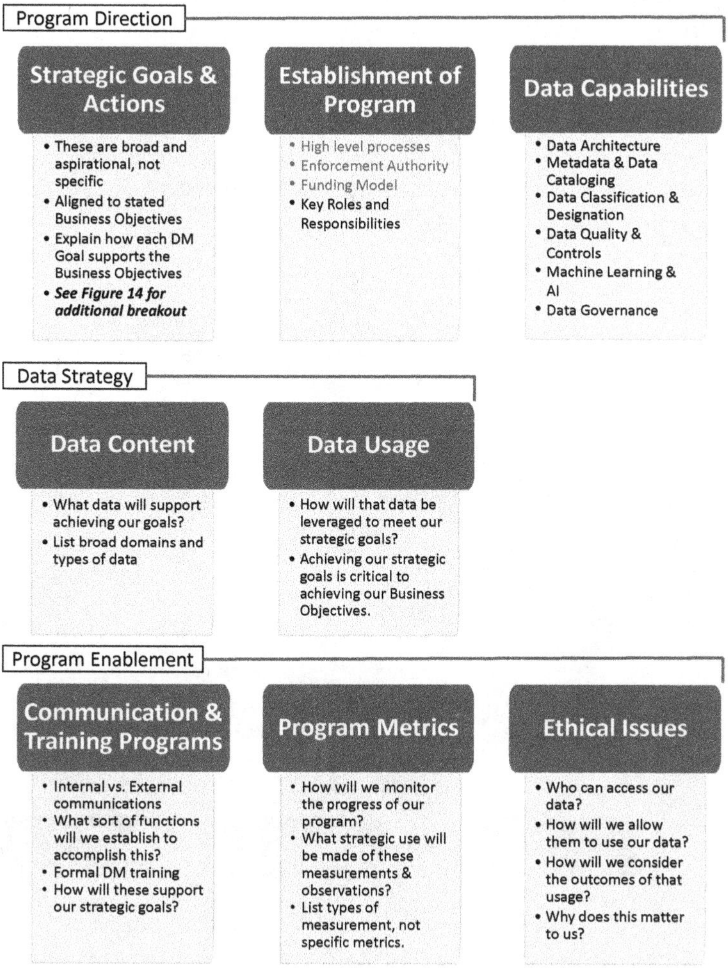

Program Direction

Strategic Goals & Actions
- These are broad and aspirational, not specific
- Aligned to stated Business Objectives
- Explain how each DM Goal supports the Business Objectives
- *See Figure 14 for additional breakout*

Establishment of Program
- High level processes
- Enforcement Authority
- Funding Model
- Key Roles and Responsibilities

Data Capabilities
- Data Architecture
- Metadata & Data Cataloging
- Data Classification & Designation
- Data Quality & Controls
- Machine Learning & AI
- Data Governance

Data Strategy

Data Content
- What data will support achieving our goals?
- List broad domains and types of data

Data Usage
- How will that data be leveraged to meet our strategic goals?
- Achieving our strategic goals is critical to achieving our Business Objectives.

Program Enablement

Communication & Training Programs
- Internal vs. External communications
- What sort of functions will we establish to accomplish this?
- Formal DM training
- How will these support our strategic goals?

Program Metrics
- How will we monitor the progress of our program?
- What strategic use will be made of these measurements & observations?
- List types of measurement, not specific metrics.

Ethical Issues
- Who can access our data?
- How will we allow them to use our data?
- How will we consider the outcomes of that usage?
- Why does this matter to us?

Figure 13: Components of Data Management Strategy.

Program Direction

Strategic Goals & Actions

Where do you want to end up? What is your Target State and what actions will you take to get there? To determine this, you'll have to do some significant analysis.

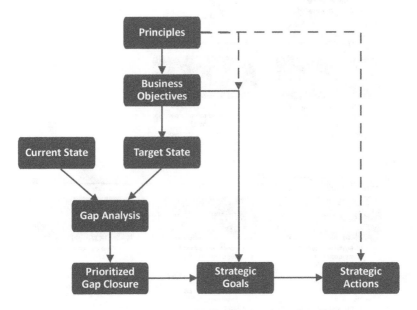

Figure 14: Determining Strategic Goals and Actions

First, you'll need to determine your Current State. One way to do this is via a Data Management Capability Assessment.[18] From there, you'll need to know where you want to be (your Target State). Remember our Business Objectives from Chapter 8? When we discussed those Objectives, we gave some examples of initiatives that Data

---

[18] Data Management Capability Assessments are discussed in more detail in Chapter 11.

Management/Data Governance might undertake to support achieving the Business Objectives. Now is the time to ask where we are relative to our ability to support the achievement of those Objectives. Ask how we would *like* to be able to support their achievement. Dig deep here—not to come up with lots of detail (remember, we are still defining a *Strategic Plan*, not a *Tactical Plan*) but rather to ensure we are clear about our current shortcomings. Be realistic about what can be accomplished over the timeframe covered by the Strategy, but do so with a "bang-for-the-buck" mentality. Consider:

- the resource dedication or effort of each initiative
- the functional value of each initiative
- the *criticality* of each initiative.

Those last two may sound like two ways of saying the same thing, but they are subtly different. An initiative can have great *value* but have little impact on achieving your Business Objectives. For example, an initiative that successfully leveraged GenAI to automatically create Business Definitions for all your Critical Data Elements would provide a lot of value to the organization. However, if none of your Strategic Goals involve metadata, such an initiative would rate low on the *criticality* scale. You needn't go into precise detail on any of these metrics—simple "tee-shirt" sizing (S/M/L) is typically adequate for the exercise.

Note that the first two metrics (ease of implementation and value) work hand-in-glove. For example, you would generally deprioritize something that required a Large amount of effort but produced a Small amount of value. The *criticality* metric, however, may override such prioritization. If that Large-effort/Small-value initiative is critical to the achievement of a particular Business Objective, it may shoot to the top of your list (one could say that the "Large" *criticality* rating essentially overrides the "Small" *value* rating (see Figure 15).

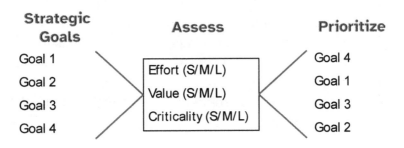

Figure 15: Prioritization of Goals

The answers to these questions constitute the basis for your Target State.

A Gap Analysis, basically a statement of what to do to turn your Current State into your Target State, comes next. For strategic purposes, this need not be a detailed analysis–the details are more of an implementation rather than a guardrail concern. You merely want to know what high-level Strategic Goals are necessary to achieve your Target State. If, for example, you identify the need for a more sophisticated analytics function in your Target State, the DMS needn't call out the details of how to implement that function. Rather, it merely needs to identify something like, "Internally managed Generative AI models using in-house Small Language Models will be leveraged to gain insights into Customer buying behavior."

You may find that you have a long list of gaps, and if so, it is important to group these into related areas and prioritize them. At a minimum, consider the effort/value/criticality ratings mentioned above. If you have an established prioritization methodology that considers additional factors, feel free to incorporate those factors as well. Once so prioritized, this list becomes your list of Target State Strategic Goals. The Goals, in turn, will require certain Strategic Actions to achieve. Depending on the complexity of each Goal, there may be one or more associated Actions (bearing in mind that some Actions may support the attainment of two or more Goals).

Whether or not you actually incorporate this current-to-target state goal analysis into your DMS, either in detail or at a summary level, is largely a matter of corporate communication style. If you do *not* include these details within the DMS, they should be made available as supplemental material (i.e., in a separate document that is referenced in the Related Documents section of your Common Matter for the DMS). What most categorically needs to be in this section of the strategy is the list of *Strategic Goals* and the *Strategic Actions* that define what types of things you'll do to achieve those Target State Strategic Goals. These Strategic Goals & Actions should be:

- Broad and aspirational, not specific
- Directly aligned to stated Business Objectives
- Clear articulations of how each DM Goal supports one or more of the Business Objectives.

This will typically give rise to statements like

> *In order to support the achievement of <Business Goal>, we will establish <Strategic Goal>*

or

> *In order to achieve <Strategic Goal>, we will perform <Strategic Action>.*

Finally, consider how your **Principles** might influence the prioritization and, perhaps, even the formulation of your Strategic Goals and Strategic Actions. Most immediately, we see our Principles reflected in our Business Objectives, but depending on the specific Principles, they may also have an influence on how the Strategic Goals and Actions are formulated.

Establishment of Program

You will need to establish a Data Management Program[19] (DMP) to execute the Data Management Strategy. This DMP may be run by a large and complex functional unit, or it may be a single compact team. What needs to be made clear within the DMS is the overall constitution of this program and why this particular "shape and size" is strategically important to achieving the Business Objectives. We don't need a lot of detail—most of that "size and shape" will be spelled out in the Data Management Operating Model (discussed in the next chapter). In this section of the DMS, we describe the primary characteristics

---

[19] The word "Program" tends to take on different meanings outside of the United States. In the US, we typically refer to an ongoing, Business-as-Usual initiative as a "program." There is an implication that such a "program" will be sustained year over year. Outside of the US, "program" is more likely to indicate a one-off initiative (what, in the US, would more typically be called a "project"). In this sense of "program," we may still be talking about a long-term initiative but it is an initiative that will have pre-defined start and end dates. Throughout this book, we will use the term "Program" in the US sense.

of the program and explain why they matter from a *business* perspective. Consider how the program will be structured to deploy Data Management in a way that most optimally leads to achieving the Business Objectives. You'll want to account for:

- **High-level processes and functions** – This is not a catalog of specific processes and procedures but rather the most fundamental kinds of things for which the DMP will be accountable. For example, overseeing execution against the DMS, monitoring compliance with established Policies and Standards, governing the use of approved taxonomies, ensuring cooperation with other Control Functions, and so forth.

- **Enforcement Authority** – This may be a simple statement like, "The Chief Data Officer will be empowered to establish whatever governance roles and committees are deemed necessary to ensure full compliance with all the mandates defined within the various Data Management guardrail documents." We might include a very high-level escalation path, but it is more typical to point to a more detailed specification that is defined elsewhere, such as, "An escalation path will be defined in detail in the Data Management Operating Model."

- **Funding Model** – A Funding Model is an overall description of all the factors that will determine funding in any given situation. It is distinct (albeit with overlaps) from the organization's overall budget request and allocation process, as we'll see in the next chapter. The details of the Funding

Model will, again, be left to the Operating Model, but the strategic importance and the reasons why we want a Funding Model belong in this section. Again, this may be a single high-level statement such as, "In order to maintain maximum stability in volatile economic periods, we will develop a Funding Model that will address funding concerns over a wide range of contingencies."

- **Key Roles and Responsibilities** – Specific role descriptions will generally be defined either in the Operating Model or in a supplemental Data Management Roles and Responsibilities Standard. What we expect to see within the DMS are statements like, "We will establish the role of Chief Data and Analytics Officer (CDAO) to ensure consistent and responsible execution against the DMS. The CDAO will be accountable for–[list accountabilities only at a very high level here]."

---

*Fundamentally, you're not **defining** these things so much as **establishing that they are important** and that they will be defined elsewhere (mostly within the Operating Model).*

Data Capabilities

A number of core Data Management capabilities will enable us to accomplish our Strategic Goals. As we will see in the next chapter (Data Management Operating Model), these will typically tie to a formal Data Capability Framework, but within the DMS, we want to call out the primary areas and set high-level strategic goals for each of them, explaining how implementing new capabilities and maturing existing capabilities will help ensure that we are well-positioned to support the business in achieving their Business Objectives. For example, state *why* a consistent Data Architecture is important to meeting these Objectives. Some additional capabilities for consideration include:

- Metadata and Data Cataloging
- Data Classification and Designation
- Data Quality and Controls
- Machine Learning and AI
- Data Governance.

This needn't (indeed, *shouldn't*) be a lengthy section. There is no need to provide details of the individual practices of each capability or to discuss specific implementation plans. Provide a brief description of what "Data Classification and Designation" (for example) might mean to you, but follow that description with no more than a sentence or two about *why* it is important to achieving your Strategic Goals.

Although this section will likely be brief, it is important because it is a primary determinant of what mandates will go into your Policy and, in turn, what Standards you will need to write (see Chapter 12).

Data Strategy

At the top of this chapter, we discussed having a Data Strategy aligned with or incorporated within the Data Management Strategy and we mentioned two components of the Data Strategy:

- The Data *Content* Strategy will identify the types of data that most directly relate to achieving our Strategic Goals (and hence, the Business Objectives).

- The Data *Usage* Strategy will describe how we intend to leverage that data to achieve those goals.

Data Content

Although the DMS, in general, will describe *why* certain structures and activities are strategically important to us, the Data Content Strategy must *identify* the broad domains of data that will be most important to achieving specific goals. *Think of this, in part, as a statement of scope for what data will be under management when we achieve our Target State.* The identification will be done at a high level—certainly no more specific than Logical Data Domains,[20] but your strategic designations may be even broader than domains. For example:

> *We will leverage real-time transactional data to engage our customers more deeply during their in-store shopping experience.*

---

[20] We will discuss Logical Data Domains in more detail in the next chapter as well as in the Glossary at the end of this book but, for our purposes right now, we will describe a Logical Data Domain (or, simply, Data Domain), as a distinct category of data content that is of interest to one or more parts of the organization. Examples include Customer Data, Product Data, Sales Data, Financial Data and so forth.

By analogy, if the identification of Critical Data Elements[21] shines a lens on specific attributes that are of prime importance to us, then the identification of these strategic Data Domains, in a sense, designates Critical Data *Classes*.

Once again, remember to think strategically here. Yes, identifying the data categories is a prime consideration for this particular strategy component. However, since it *is* a strategy, explaining *why* it is deemed critical is equally important.

Data Usage

This section describes how to leverage those Critical Data Classes to meet our strategic goals (and hence, our Business Objectives). Such descriptions may include the technologies used, such as "We will leverage Machine Learning/AI to more accurately predict customer buying habits." We will not necessarily describe detailed implementation initiatives. As with the identification of the content, remember that even though you are identifying specific "how's," you are doing so to describe how this will help achieve your Business Objectives. Ensure that you are clear about whether you're following some specific path in order to pursue the "new bright and shiny thing" or because it's viewed as essential to achieving a fundamental Business Objective. In most cases, you should throw away things in the first category and enshrine those in the latter. Political expediency may sometimes compel you to include the

---

[21] A Critical Data Element (CDE) is a Data Element which is a primary input to or output of a Critical Business Process. CDE's are generally defined at the Business or Logical Level and so may have multiple physical instantiations across the data ecosystem. See the Glossary for additional clarification.

former use cases, but ensure they are not at odds with the true business objectives (see Figure 16).

Functionality	Why	Approve?
➢GenAI	➢Everybody's doing it	✗
➢Predictive Analytics with Alternative Data	➢Identify new market segments	✓
➢Automate classification of Data Sensitivity	➢Regulatory mandate	✓

Figure 16: Selecting Data Use Cases

Exactly *how* we will use the data may or may not be unique for each identified Critical Data Class. For example, each particular class might be leveraged in a single way to achieve a specific goal (as in the example we gave above that "We will leverage real-time transactional data to give our customers a new level of engagement during their in-store shopping experience.") or we may have broader types of usage in mind. For example:

> *To improve our customers' trust in our handling of their data, we will enact increased privacy rules around any and all data related to the Customer, their interactions with us, their level of satisfaction with us, and any analysis of their ongoing relationship with us. We will do this regardless of whether the specific data includes Personally Identifiable Information or bears a more indirect relationship with the customer.*

Depending on how "one-to-one" the association is between the just-defined Critical Data Classes and these declarations of "how we will leverage the classes," you may wish to incorporate the Data Usage Strategy directly into the Data Content Strategy. For example, we might expand our "exploitation of real-time transactional data" example to read:

> *We will leverage real-time transactional data to target instant rewards at high-volume sales locations to give our customers a new level of engagement in the shopping experience.*

Program Enablement

While the strategic categories we covered so far should not be too foreign to anyone who's either constructed or at least perused a Data Management Strategy, what I called the "Program Enablers" in Figure 13 might seem like surprising components for a Data Management Strategy. The three components in this section (Communications and Training, Data Metrics and Ethical Issues) all deal with the empowerment of our staff and the measurement of the progress they are making.

Communications and Training

If we place any emphasis on the importance of *people* in achieving our business goals, then how we communicate with them (whether "them" means our employees, our customers, our regulators, or even the general public) takes on very specific strategic value. What and how we need to communicate with our staff presents distinctly different concerns than do our communications with external bodies (shareholders, the general public, regulators, etc.) and the strategic value propositions will be distinctly different. To that end, I recommend that the DMS say something about the *strategic importance* of these areas in achieving your Strategic Goals.

There are some general factors you'll want to think about:

- Will you establish a formal Communications department within the Data Management function or simply communicate via the standard Corporate Communications organization (if, indeed, you have one)?

- What sort of oversight will you have over the communications? For example, will you monitor employees' social media postings to ensure they are not exposing important information?

At the risk of repeating myself, I want to stress once again that this is *not* the place to define the specifics of *how* you will communicate or train your people. You are not crafting a Communication Plan or a Training Curriculum, but rather defining the *strategic importance* of doing these things.

Communications

Internal communications

Internal communications encompass everything from Data Management or Data Issues that will impact some part of the organization to broadcasting general "wins" in the Data space. It will also include a wide range of status reporting. Audiences will vary from a handful of senior executives to the entire organization, including employees, contractors and on-site vendors. When identifying the ways in which your communications will provide strategic value, consider questions like the following:

- What is the strategic value of communicating within the organization?

- Do different types of communication support different strategic goals?

- Will the CDO hold regular "town hall" meetings with the Data Management Team?

- Will stakeholders outside the DM practitioners be included in these meetings?

- Why do we consider it important to communicate certain types of information to the broad organization?

- What about a "two-way street?" What kind of input is important for management to solicit from the broader organization?

- Will we invest in infrastructure to facilitate this communication (e.g., development of a corporate-wide DM Portal to keep the whole company abreast of what DM is accomplishing vis-à-vis the achievement of our Business Objectives)?

External communications

External audiences vary greatly and can include your shareholders, your customers, the general public, regulatory bodies (if applicable to your industry) and numerous subsets of all those categories. Remember, still, that you are focused on identifying *strategic value* (as opposed to any kind of specific communication plan). In addition to all the questions you asked about your internal audiences, also consider:

- Through what kinds of channels will you share with these people?

- How forthcoming will you be about changes to how you manage data? You may well have legal obligations to disclose certain things, but will you do the bare minimum of disclosure, or will you go the extra mile to explain things in detail?[22]

- Think about how forthcoming you'll be about delivering "bad news," such as what you'll tell your customers when you have a data breach (and, sad to say, I'm afraid that the operative word these days is "when" rather than "if").

Training

In order to ensure a common degree of understanding across all your Data stakeholders, it is frequently necessary to establish some degree of training for those stakeholders. Different stakeholders will have different needs in this regard. Some will be active practitioners who are directly involved in the production, maintenance or governance of our data. Others will be less "hands-on" stakeholders who, nonetheless, need to consume that data.

---

[22] A particularly current topic that illustrates the strategic value of your communications is whether you plan to use customer information to train your Language Models. For some customers, this may be unacceptable to them and they may choose to take their business elsewhere if you tell them this. However, if you do *not* tell them, they may be even more likely to leave once they find out (and, if you don't tell them, eventually someone else *will*!). Your strategy needs to consider such factors.

The appropriate method for the delivery of this wide range of training is also likely to vary. For intensive, practitioner-specific skills, you may commit to forming a partnership with a local college or university to enable interested staff to obtain valuable skills that would be difficult and/or expensive to achieve internally. At the other extreme, perhaps you may establish a series of in-house e-learning seminars that will familiarize your stakeholders with the fundamentals of Data Management and the associated Guiding Principles (See Chapter 7).

As with our Communications Strategy, a reminder that this section is not where you would define the specifics of what you will do. You are not spelling out a Training Curriculum, but rather, you are defining the strategic importance of doing these things. In fact, this section of our Strategy may consist of a single strategic goal, such as *"We will continue to invest in the ongoing training of our staff to improve the retention of our most valuable talent by ensuring they feel they have a clear growth path within XYZ Corp."*

Program Metrics

We will discuss the actual definition of Metrics, in varying degrees of specificity, in some of the remaining sections of the guardrail hierarchy, but first, let's look at the strategic relevance of assessing how we're doing. Remembering that we are now defining a *strategy*, I'll reiterate that, within this document, we are not talking about a list of specific measurements but rather about the *kinds* of measurements that will help ensure that we are on track to achieve our strategic goals. At the risk of being redundant, I want to emphasize the importance of thinking strategically rather than tactically in this section. We want to focus on questions like:

- How will we monitor the progress of our program vis-à-vis our strategic goals?

- What strategic use will we make of these measurements and observations?

- Are there some types of "aspirational" metrics that could be of strategic importance to us? "Aspirational" in the sense that, although we may not know exactly how to calculate such types right now, they would provide useful information if we *could* calculate them. Avoid the highly impractical, but consider what *might* be possible.

Typical statements in this section will be along the lines of:

- "In order to help achieve the goal of improved customer satisfaction, we will develop continuous monitoring of social media and produce a comprehensive set of end-of-day metrics on trending public sentiment."

- "In order to ensure the successful roll-out of our new Generative AI practice, we will publish monthly statistics related to the status of all significant Language Model-informed initiatives."

- "In order to ensure that our new Data Management Issue Escalation process is working effectively, senior data governance officials will be provided with a dashboard showing real-time statistics on all open and recently resolved DM issues."

Ethical Concerns

The question of data ethics has become an increasingly hot topic in recent years, in no small part driven by the meteoric rise of ungoverned (not to mention widely misunderstood) use of generative AI in many companies. How is the ethical use of data (GenAI-related or otherwise) potentially strategic? Let's first take a moment to define what we mean by ethics in general and data ethics in particular.

You can find many formal definitions of Data Ethics on the internet, but I think it's more compelling just to review some of the "off-the-cuff" definitions I've heard from a number of Data Governance Officers and their advisors and colleagues over the years:

- *Data Ethics is what guides us when nobody's watching.*

- *Data Ethics means using data in a way that respects the dignity of the individual.*

- *Data Ethics means **not** using data in any way in which we would not want **our** data to be used.*

- *Ethical use of Data means never engaging in activities at which we would not want to be caught (!)*[23]

Depending on where your organization does business, you will find that the Ethical Use of Data only partially overlaps with the *Legal* Use of Data. Different jurisdictions around the world have different views on acceptable uses of data,

---

[23] For those of you old enough to get the reference, I once heard somebody express this same sentiment as "Data Ethics means never having to say you're sorry." (See https://en.wikipedia.org/wiki/Love_Story_(1970_film) if you're not old enough.)

so the degree of overlap may be very small or quite significant. It is, of course, incumbent upon our various levels of internal oversight to be highly aware of those legal requirements. Cross-jurisdictional requirements may be complex, but at least such legal mandates are documented somewhere. At present, especially in the United States, the question of "What is Ethical?" tends to be more organization-dependent. Most modern companies indeed have some kind of general Code of Ethical Behavior, and some of these Codes may have ramifications for data and information security. But a formal Code of Data Ethics (which may be a separate document or part of a general Code of Ethics) focuses specifically on the ethical ramifications of who can access data, what use can be made of that data once accessed, and what the outcomes of using that data in a particular way might be.

The Data Management Strategy is no place to state your formal Code of Data Ethics (indeed, if you have such a documented Code, it may well be owned by a Control Function other than Data Management). However, there is distinct *strategic* value in addressing the importance of ethical use of data. Depending on your overall Business Objectives, these may be quite obvious. For example, returning to our recurring example Objective of "Improve Customer Satisfaction," that's a goal that would benefit from having a well-publicized and enforced Code of Data Ethics that talks about what we will and won't do with the Customer's Data (*regardless* of what we are *legally* required to do or not to do). This can be great Public Relations, even if it seems to constrain our ability to perform data-related activities that would make our corporate life easier.[24] For example, it might be easier to identify new target markets by using "borderline unethical" (albeit legally permitted) mining of our customers' data. But what might the impact on our Market Share be if this data mining became known to the public? Would potential customers care? Do we care if they care? Would it impact our ability to attract the new customers we identified through our somewhat questionable techniques? There's no "one-size-fits-all" answer here, so how will we address the question from a strategic standpoint?

While Data Ethics, especially as it relates to our Data Management Strategy, is tightly coupled with the highly organization-specific notion of Data Risk Appetite,[25] we can, in general, say that ethical use of data can play a significant role in mitigating our exposure to legal risk (much, if not all, that is unethical is also illegal), reputational risk (you don't want the public thinking that you have no respect for their personal information) and regulatory risk (as data privacy regulations proliferate more and more, an increasing number of organizations are

---

[24] If you doubt the strategic value of doing things that you're not legally required to do, consider a certain hot dog company who, in one of the longest-running ad campaigns ever, stated, "The Government says that we can put <long list of additives> in our hot dogs...but we answer to a higher authority." (For a more detailed description of the history of this advertising campaign, refer to https://en.wikipedia.org/wiki/We_answer_to_a_higher_authority).

[25] For those unfamiliar with this term, Data Risk Appetite (often defined in a Data Risk Appetite Statement) is basically just the company's position on "Is X worth the risk?" In short, it is an expression of how willing we are to undertake an activity that exposes us to some degree of risk, given that the associated "risky" behavior may facilitate the achievement of some goal. This is discussed in more detail in the Glossary.

under greater scrutiny for how they are using their customers' data).

If your organization has one or more Business Strategies, these may include language addressing the strategic value of ethical behavior in general. This language can serve as fodder for how the Data Management Strategy will incorporate Data Ethics into achieving the organization's strategic goals.

Once again, the Data Management Strategy is no place to *state* your formal Code of Data Ethics but I feel it is a mistake to ignore the *strategic* value of a strong approach to Data Ethics when formulating your Strategy. This is where you get to explain how the ethical use of data is important to achieving your strategic goals. Some key questions to consider are:

- Who can ethically access our data?

- How will we allow them to use our data?

- How will we consider the outcomes of that usage?

- Why does this matter to us?

- How does it support the achievement of our Strategic Goals and, by extension, our Business Objectives?

The first three bullets are, in effect, our "scratch-pad." Once we've determined answers to these questions from a Data Ethics viewpoint, these become input for answering the questions in the last two bullets. What we come up with for those answers will, most fundamentally, constitute the statement of our Data Ethics strategy.

Category	Strategic
Name	DM Strategy
Description	A statement of approach and prioritization for how the DM function will support the achievement of the Business Objectives.
What	**HOW** WE'LL GET THERE
Sample Level of Specificity	"To ensure consistent understanding of our data, we will establish an enterprise-wide data catalog."
Characteristics	Directional, Aligned to Business Objective; Accountability lies with leadership.

Table 4: Characteristics of Data Management Strategy

TEN

Governance Guardrails

As we move through the high-level, three-part grouping of our Guardrail Documents, we now reach the middle grouping of Governance-related guardrails. These are the document types that first come to mind for most people when we speak of Data Governance. In the next two chapters, we will examine the document types that most immediately control our Data Governance and Data Management activities and that will define the structures and mandates that allow us to execute those activities in a manner that most effectively supports achieving our Strategic Goals and Activities.

- We propose a very comprehensive **Data Management Operating Model** that addresses not only the organizational and governance structures we will develop but also the high-level structuring of our data, the adoption of a Capability Framework, and various other structures that ensure we operate consistently across our entire data ecosystem.

- We will examine **Data Management Policies** and **Standards** in a single chapter because we propose a far more integrated approach to these critical Data Governance Guardrail Documents than is often employed.

As we venture into these waters that are at once conceptually very familiar and yet interpretationally potentially quite murky, we may encounter organizationally imposed constraints on just how closely the approaches I propose would be allowed. I have helped multiple clients develop Operating Models and Policy/Standards that follow the approach laid out here, and these have been highly successful. However, you may find that one or more of the following impede your ability to implement the formats covered in this book:

- Corporate culture
- Policy documentation standards or protocols
- Policy approval processes
- Legacy policy structure and/or operating model(s).

To that end, I will suggest workarounds for some of the impediments you are most likely to encounter and, additionally, will try to encapsulate the underlying concepts and reasoning behind my recommendations in the hope that these can help you evolve a methodology for applying these concepts to your particular environment.

Figure 17: Governance Guardrails

ELEVEN

Data Management Operating Model

How Data Management will be structured to meet the Strategic Objectives.

Acomprehensive Data Management Operating Model is a key artifact in defining how the DM/DG initiative will be structured to fulfill the goals of the Data Management Strategy. It establishes the structure, scope, and coverage of the different parts of Data Management and designs how they should work together to serve the needs of the business. As an operationalization of the Data Management Strategy, it should go without saying that it must be closely aligned with that Strategy and be created with a specific focus on what structures are optimally supportive of fulfilling the goals of the Strategy.

The Operating Model is the responsibility of the Chief Data Office although accountability will frequently be assigned to one or more of the CDO's senior staff. As always, we should solicit input from all concerned stakeholder groups.

In the Data Management Strategy, we allowed for "supplemental" strategies within the various Operating Units. The Operating Model, by contrast, is meant to present a comprehensive, all-inclusive view of the Data Management organization. As an example, if we consider our definition of the key Data Management roles, the Operating Units can decide the *details* according to their needs (such as the number of individuals to place in a specific role or whether a single individual may cover two or more roles), but we should define the roles themselves at the Enterprise level. If specific Operating Units have highly specific structural needs (such as an OU-specific role), the definitions of these structures should be incorporated into the Enterprise Operating Model with the appropriate qualifiers. Such qualifiers would typically be in the form of an optionality statement rather than tying the role hard and fast to a specific Operating Unit. At some point in the future, that role could become relevant to other Operating Units, and defining the role as distinct from a particular Operating Unit's current needs helps protect the sustainability of the Operating Model.

Specificity

The Operating Model documentation varies significantly from most of our other guardrail documents in that it is not particularly "statement" oriented. We are defining *structures,* and, as we are about to see, many sections of the Operating Model are highly amenable to being expressed graphically (perhaps with a handful of some associated text to clarify things). To speak of degrees of specificity is not entirely meaningful in these cases. It is more a question of the *level* of specificity in our structural definitions.

How detailed these definitions should be will depend, in no small part, on the complexity of the defined structures. In general, my advice is that the definitions should be precise but not *necessarily* detailed. For example, when defining a Data Governance structure, you should define the appropriate governing bodies, the high-level responsibilities of each body, the primary roles that will sit on the body, and the associated escalation path(s) for issue resolution (this is roughly analogous to the reporting hierarchy of the Organizational Structure). Do NOT get into details of how often each body should meet, what their agendas should cover, or what processes they will follow. Such details will either be defined elsewhere (such as the Process documentation) or decided by each body. Remember that you are defining *structures,* not processes or general activities.

Because the Operating Model is an extension of the Data Management Strategy, some companies like to incorporate it directly into their Strategy document, especially if their Operating Model is fairly simple. However, I believe it is worth defining the Operating Model in a separate document to make it more accessible and to highlight it as the *operationalization* of the Data Management Strategy.

Why Does this Matter?

As stated above, the primary intent of the Operating Model is to define the structures that will allow for the successful implementation of the Data Management function. It defines the configurations of people, tools, and data that will most readily and robustly support the performance of the Strategic Actions laid out in the Data Management Strategy and that will create a coherently integrated Data Management Organization.

Why does this Belong in our Hierarchy?

The Operating Model, in some respects, fits rather tenuously into the definition of a Guardrail. It is more of an implementation specification than a mandate, constraint, or guideline. However, insofar as it defines how we will structure the organization to fulfill our Strategic Goals and to comply with our Data Management Policy,[26] it is very relevant to our Guardrail Hierarchy. We have already stated that it is an extension of the DMS (indeed, in some companies, it is actually **part** of the DMS). For all these reasons, we place the Operating Model squarely within the Guardrail Hierarchy to ensure that we understand its role in our Holistic Data Governance initiative.

---

[26] Data Management Policies will be discussed in detail in the next chapter.

What Content Belongs in the Data Management Operating Model?

Like the DMS, the Operating Model has several distinct sections. Individually and collectively, these sections:

- Formalize the adoption of a Capability Model so that you have a clear vision of sustainable target-state Data Management. A Capability Model is a framework that specifies a methodology and approach that will serve as the Data Management Capability target state for the Data Management function.

- Establish a model for organizing your data to ensure a consistent understanding of the data categories that are most important to fulfilling your goals. This model should represent the logical boundaries of data *across* business domains as well as the relationships between and accountabilities for data domains and (optionally) data products.

- Define accountabilities and responsibilities to ensure everyone understands their part in obtaining maximum value from the organization's data. This structure describes the various Data Management roles, their primary responsibilities, and their relationship to one another.

- Define a Data Governance structure to ensure an effective means of oversight and a clear escalation path for resolving issues. This structure describes the hierarchy of roles, groups, or committees that define, oversee or adjudicate matters of compliance and issue management.

- Define a Data Management Tool Stack with known capabilities and future requirements so that you can make informed investments in technology. This model represents the current state software infrastructure with identified high-level functional requirements for achieving a target state.

- Establish the formal approach for funding the Data Management function in all foreseeable scenarios (BAU, projects, day-to-day operations, various types of disruptions) to ensure the best position for sustaining the Data Management Program in good times and bad. This model describes the various scenarios the organization may encounter and specifies how to seek funding in each of those scenarios.

- Establish a foundation for driving a culture that values data as an asset so that everyone from the C-Suite to new hires has a shared vision and a full appreciation of how important they, as individuals, are to the effective management of the organization's data. This approach ensures data literacy and the adoption of data accountability through comprehensive training and communication.

- Establish objective measurements for assessing progress to provide a clear understanding of achievement. This is a high-level specification of the *types* of metrics that will be used to measure the DM Program's success in meeting the Strategic Goals and, in turn, the Business Objectives.

We can express this more concisely in the following image:

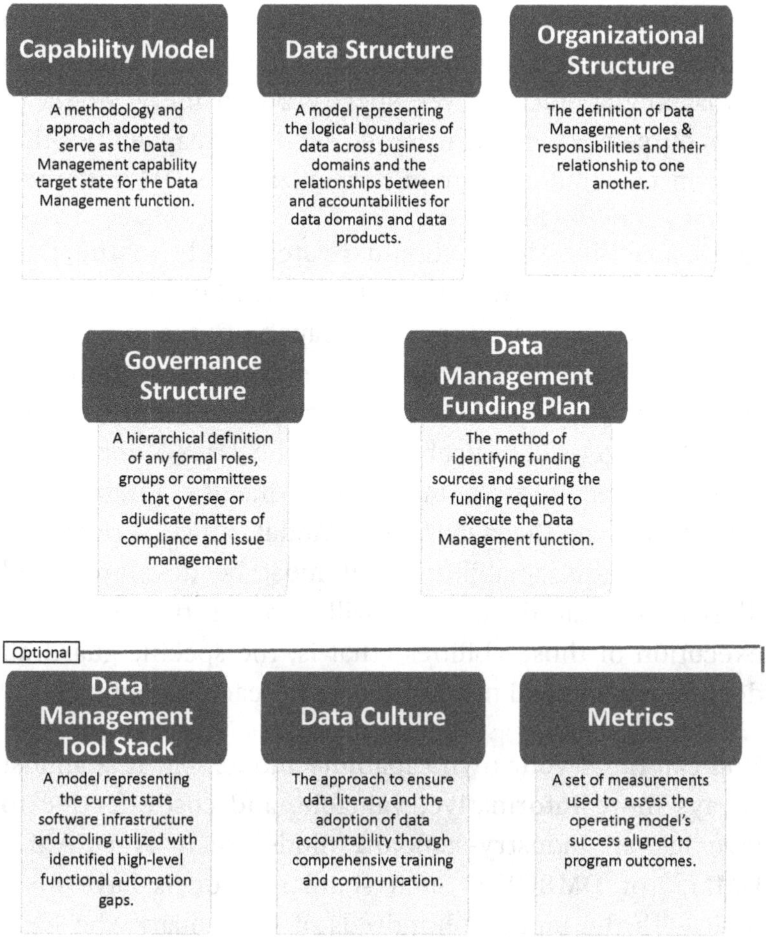

Capability Model

A methodology and approach adopted to serve as the Data Management capability target state for the Data Management function.

Data Structure

A model representing the logical boundaries of data across business domains and the relationships between and accountabilities for data domains and data products.

Organizational Structure

The definition of Data Management roles & responsibilities and their relationship to one another.

Governance Structure

A hierarchical definition of any formal roles, groups or committees that oversee or adjudicate matters of compliance and issue management

Data Management Funding Plan

The method of identifying funding sources and securing the funding required to execute the Data Management function.

Optional

Data Management Tool Stack

A model representing the current state software infrastructure and tooling utilized with identified high-level functional automation gaps.

Data Culture

The approach to ensure data literacy and the adoption of data accountability through comprehensive training and communication.

Metrics

A set of measurements used to assess the operating model's success aligned to program outcomes.

Figure 18: Components of the Data Management Operating Model

Capability Model

A *Data Management Capability* is a defined and demonstrated ability to accomplish a specific Data Management task or set of tasks in a repeatable fashion. A Data Management Capability Model, then, is a framework that defines the set of capabilities deemed necessary to support the implementation of a comprehensive Data Management practice. We specify a Capability Model to align ourselves with an accepted set of DM capabilities that we consider important to our organization's DM initiative.

The Capability Model should relate closely to the Data Capabilities outlined in the Strategy (in fact, some of my clients have addressed the Data Capability section of their Strategy simply by embedding a reference to an industry-standard Capability Model). This model will represent the desired target-state capabilities of the Data Management function and, in so doing, will define the fundamental activities that the Operating Model must support. It represents the capabilities that must be developed and illustrates what documents will support the consistent execution of those abilities (that is, the specific guardrail documents you will need to create for each capability).

You can build your own capability model, but it is almost always more informative, valuable, and cost-effective to leverage an industry-standard model such as DCAM,[27] DMM,[28] or DMBOK.[29] Such standard models have been built with the input of hundreds of individuals who have shared their own experiences and those of their respective

---

[27] The Data Management Capability Assessment Model (DCAM) is the intellectual property of the EDM Council. For more information, see https://edmcouncil.org/frameworks/dcam.

[28] The Data Management Maturity Model (DMM) is the intellectual property of CMMI. For more information, see https://cmmiinstitute.com/cmmi/.

[29] The Data Management Book of Knowledge (DMBOK or DMBoK) is the intellectual property of DAMA International. For more information, see https://www.dama.org/cpages/body-of-knowledge.

employers. Many of these models include a standard assessment methodology, and some maintain a database of industry benchmark results for comparison purposes. Using such a widely-sourced model (as opposed to building your own) allows you to:

- Leverage industry-standard and tested capability frameworks and best practices that can accelerate the delivery of data value.

- Standardize on a common language for discussing Data and Analytics Management to ensure that conflicting terminology does not hinder understanding.

- Establish a consistent capability assessment methodology, allowing for gap analysis and strategic roadmaps.

- Compare capability achievements to industry peers so that you can objectively assess your strategic advantage in the marketplace.

Data Structure

The Data Structure portion of the Operating Model addresses the high-level ways you'll organize your data ecosystem. When we speak of *Data Structure* within the Operating Model, we primarily look at a high-level definition of **logical data domains**. The easiest way to conceptualize your data domains is to list the ways you *think* about your data.

Figure 19: Thinking about Data Domains

Whereas the DMS described *why* specific domains or of data were of particular importance to us, the Operating Model will provide a comprehensive list of our Logical Data Domains. We do not tie these to specific physical repositories at this point. The Data Architecture team typically performs that activity after the domains are defined. In the Operating Model, we merely define them as categories. While you want the list to be comprehensive, do not obsess over accounting for every last data element in your organization. Some data will be transitory or related to operational workspaces and may or may not fall neatly into any of your Logical Data Domains. Focus on the domains that are meaningful to the business. Very often, this will mean types of data that are shared across two or more Operating Units.

Once agreed to with your key stakeholders, these categories become your Logical Data Domains. These Data Domains establish the high-level boundaries of data across your business and help you:

- Organize the data ecosystem, clarifying the scope of data under management.

- Identify boundary criteria for data subsets, providing a methodological underpinning for maintaining the domains.

- Address data requirements across the organization, providing an organization-wide data structure that works for both local and central processes.

- Establish a foundation for data accountability, defining the granularity of data ownership across the organization.[30]

There's no one right way to do this—much depends on the structure of your organization and the nature of your business. Data domains aren't physical repositories or databases. They're logical categories of data that are deemed important to your normal business operation. Whatever data domains you establish, to get full value out of them, they must be identified, defined, inventoried, and used consistently throughout the organization. Since domains often represent data that is shared across different parts of the organization, often with competing claims on ownership, it can be advantageous to assign a Domain Data Steward (or some other cross-Operating-Unit role) who can take ultimate accountability for integrating the data within the domain into a reconciled whole, regardless of where it originated.

In some particularly complicated data landscapes, defining sub-domains (as shown under Customer and Product in

---

[30] The title of "Data Owner" can be contentious in some organizations and I will not attempt to address the finer points of who does or should "own" the data. For purposes of our discussion, when we speak of data ownership, we refer, most fundamentally, to the identification of the person who has ultimate responsibility for the data and its definition.

Figure 20) may make sense. In rare cases, there *might* be value in establishing sub-sub-domains, but use these sparingly, if at all. The true value of managing data in domains is to ensure maximal consistency. If you subdivide a domain into too many sub-categories, you lose much of the unifying value inherent in domain-based management of the data.

No matter how many domains you define, remember that this cross-Operating-Unit unification is one of the primary benefits of domain management, and *that* is why it is important to make Data Domains part of your Operating Model.

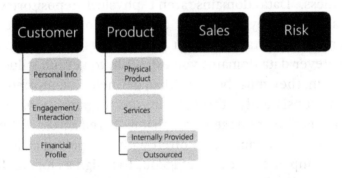

Figure 20: Logical Data Domain example

 Figure 20 is a very abbreviated example. Your actual set of domains will, most likely, have significantly more entries. While I've tried to make the examples in this chapter meaningful, this is one of the constructs (Figure 23, Figure 25, and Figure 28 are more cases) where the definitions required in a real-life Operating Model would become too lengthy to use as brief illustrations in this book.

Contrast with Other Types of Domains

I have found over the years that many organizations that claim to manage their data in a data domain structure are actually managing according to Business or Functional domains. Business Domains, rather than being based on data content, reflect what the various Business Units need to do with their data. While these Business Units **do** have data that is specific to their part of the overall business, they also access data that is common across multiple (often across all) Business Units (Customer being a prime example). The alignment of data to these domains is based more on the services or products that each Business Unit provides rather than on what the data *means*. In my experience, this is the most common misapplication of managing data in Data Domains (see Figure 21).

Functional domains are a step further removed from any particular, meaning-derived data domains. Where Business Domain-based data partitions reflect actual data specific to a single part of the organization, Functional Domains are based on the *type* of data leveraged by some part of the organization to perform specific operational functions throughout the organization.

In any given domain, Business Domains may look quite similar to Functional Domains, but the alignment of any particular Functional Domain to one or more sets of data will be based more on what the Functional Area needs to do rather than what the data *means* (again, refer to Figure 21).

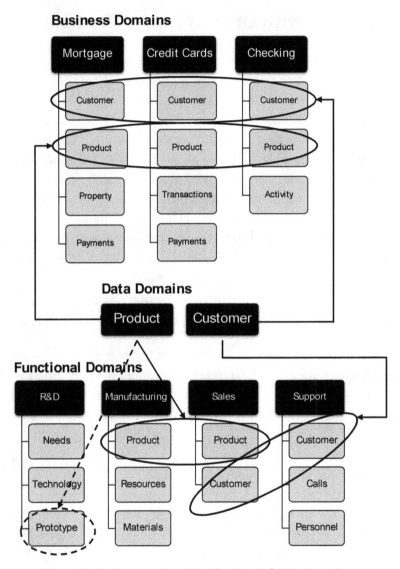

Figure 21: Business vs Functional vs Logical Data Domains

This is not simply an academic exercise in semantics. Ultimately, if you truly **adopt** a Data Domain-based approach to managing your data, understanding where data exists across your organization allows you to accurately identify the System of Record and to know who has ultimate ownership of that data. If a customer opens a checking account, are they a *customer,* or are they a *checking account customer*? Who's accountable for maintaining that customer data? Do you reconcile it to a Customer Master Record? If not, how do you know that the Jack Jones who's had a checking account with you for five years just applied for a credit card? Has he become a new customer, or does he remain an existing customer? How willing are you to risk giving Mr. Jones the impression that you have no idea he's been a loyal customer for five years? Aside from this exposure to reputational risk, there can be a further financial risk if Mr. Jones decides he'd rather do business with your competitor, who can reconcile Mr. Jones' multiple relationships with *their* company and, more than just recognize this, to actively reward him for his loyalty.

There are both business concerns and technical challenges when addressing these questions, so carefully consider how you define your data domains.

Organizational Structure

In most organizations, the Enterprise Data Management/Data Governance function defines the guardrail documents with which the Local Data Management functions must comply. This sort of Federated approach[31] is what we're illustrating in Figure 22. Note that your approach may differ.

Of course, it's usually not quite that clear-cut. For example, although Control Functions exist at the Enterprise level, like Business Units, they must comply with the Enterprise mandates. When we define the Organizational Structure, the Control Functions will behave much like any other Operating Unit, even though they are nominally autonomous functions. As such, we must define the *centralized* roles that are most important to the Enterprise's activities as well as those that are most important at the localized Operating Unit (even if the "local" Operating Unit is, in fact, an Enterprise Control Function).

It may or may not be obvious, but the Central (Enterprise) roles will mostly be "single-position" roles (e.g., there will be one Chief Data Officer, one Head of Data Governance, and so forth—you can already see that most of these roles will have words like "Chief" or "Head of" in their titles) and the OU-specific roles will typically have **at least** one person filling that role in each Operating Unit. Large OU's may have multiple instances of the same role, such as multiple Business Data Stewards or multiple Data Architects. Even if all the Operating Units have, for example, a single Executive Data Steward, that means, at this level, that we will have multiple Executive Data Stewards (one for each Operating Unit).

---

[31] Federated vs Centralized vs Decentralized organizational structures were discussed in Chapter 1.

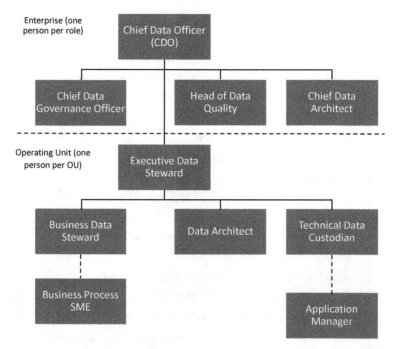

Figure 22: Organizational Structure example

Figure 22 is an example of what an organizational structure chart might look like. Of course, you may have more or fewer defined roles than the example. Remember that some roles may be performed by multiple individuals (a large Operating Unit may have two or more Technical Data Stewards, for example), and some individuals may play multiple roles (a small Operating Unit might have a single individual performing the roles of both Technical Data Steward and Data Architect). It is important, therefore, to understand the time commitment involved with each role so that you don't over-allocate responsibilities. It's worth underscoring that assigning too many accountabilities to any particular individual is an invitation to burnout, failure, and, eventually, attrition.

> ### *It's All Too Much!!!*
>
> A number of years ago, I started working with a client that was just beginning to establish their Data Governance function. One of the first roles they decided they needed was that of the Data Steward. They had very little budget available so they had been adding more and more accountabilities to this one role. They then asked someone in each Business Unit to step into that role...IN THEIR SPARE TIME!!!! The results ranged from one person who took every opportunity to let people know how unsuited he was for the role to the poor woman who actually tried to keep up until she finally requested a transfer to a different part of the organization. By overloading the role definition with too many accountabilities and then foisting the role on people with inadequate bandwidth, management was practically begging their people to fail. (The story DOES have a happy ending–eventually, the company sought (and received) funding for full-time Data Steward positions, and this became the basis for what evolved into a highly effective Data Governance operation!)

It will probably be left to Human Resources to craft detailed descriptions of each of these roles, but it is useful for the Operating Model to include a high-level RACI/RASCI or a textural description summarizing the core responsibilities of each of these roles. The intent is not to define every single role in the Data Management organization. Indeed, you may not be able to...depending on the nature of your business, other Control Functions may mandate that certain roles that *they* have defined must be staffed within the DM organization. Remember that what you want to establish is the fundamental Data Management roles that are most critical to fulfilling the Data Management Strategy.

Governance Structure

At first glance, this may seem redundant to the Organizational Structure we just discussed. After all, we saw a number of roles listed in the previous example that, based on their names alone, had obvious Data Governance responsibilities. However, the Organizational Structure concerns itself with defining individual roles. When we look at our Governance Structure, we want to define the hierarchy of governing bodies that we intend to establish.

Having an effective Data Management Governance Structure allows an organization to make definitive and consistent decisions about its Data and Data Management. The definition of this structure should include:

- Defining the various councils, committees, or other bodies overseeing compliance with the various Data Governance guardrails and adjudicating any compliance exception requests or outright compliance infractions.

- The group or groups responsible for the creation and maintenance of the Data Governance Guardrail documents.

- The *roles* (**not** the individuals) expected to sit in each of these bodies.

- The primary governance responsibilities of each body.

- The escalation path for issues that the governing body cannot resolve at the level at which the Issue arose.

It is expected that there will also be (at minimum) a formal guardrail approval process and an Issue Management process defined elsewhere. The Operating Model should reference these processes if they already exist. If they do not already exist, one or more of the bodies should be responsible for creating such processes.

 Figure 23 shows a comprehensive but fairly straightforward structure that, at least in theory, would be suitable for many mid-sized to large organizations. Some companies may have additional layers of oversight. For example, you may require a specific focus on your data domains or on various functional areas, such as Analytics or Data Ethics.

You may also find that you have two or more parallel governance structures. For example, your governance function will, at minimum:

- Author Guardrail documents
- Oversee compliance with those documents
- Adjudicate non-compliance issues.

Depending on the mandates of your organization, you may have slightly different governance bodies and/or reporting/escalation paths associated with these different activities.

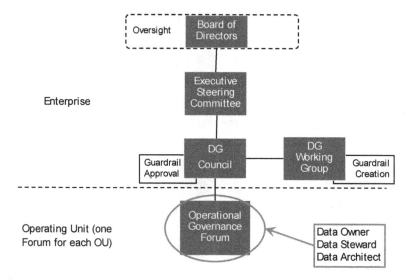

Figure 23: Governance Structure example

It should be clear that there is no one "right way" to define your Governance Structure. The important thing is that your structure works within your organizational culture and that you address:

- How to consistently direct and oversee that data management is being performed in compliance with the established guardrails.

- Ensure that you have appropriate subject matter expertise and appropriate **authority** at each level of oversight.

- Ensure that cross-level communication takes place on an appropriate basis.

Notice that I've included the Board of Directors at the top of this Governance Structure. Obviously, this group is situated outside of the Data Management/Data Governance organization, and, in many companies, it would be highly unusual for Data Management issues to escalate that high, but it **can** happen. Especially in heavily regulated industries like Financial Services and certain branches of the Life Sciences, it is not at all unknown for regulatory violations to result in recurring fines of many millions of dollars—something that the Board will **definitely** want to see resolved as quickly as possible. Even in companies with less likelihood of such extreme escalation, be clear just how high an issue **might** go and plan accordingly. It's better to have your escalation process ready to address all eventualities, even if the triggering event seems highly unlikely.

Data Management Funding Model

Oddly, as important as funding is to any operation (not just Data Management), very few people address it through a formal Funding Model. A Funding Model is not a budget request process (although the two are related). It is not about how much money you'll get for a project or even *if* you'll get money for a project. Rather, the funding model describes *how* you'll request funding in any particular eventuality and what you'll do if you don't get as much as you need. Amongst other things, this means being able to answer questions like:

- How do I "keep the lights on?"
- How do I seek funding for a high-priority "one-off" project?
- How do I pay for my technology needs?

- What do I do when there's some kind of major disruption to my ability to operate? Examples include a natural disaster, a pandemic like COVID, or an unanticipated mandate from a regulatory agency.

In general, it means knowing what channels to go through no matter *what* happens.

The Data Management Funding Model is a *framework* rather than a formal plan designed to describe how you will seek the funds allocated to DM-related operations, projects, and activities. Not only does it help set the expectations for funding across a full range of scenarios, it will also serve as an outline of the *types* of scenarios that might occur, and in identifying processes for handling them, it provides an important part of defining your operational risk. Define this framework independently of (but in alignment with) your organization's annual budgeting process. This will help you:

- Support your normal Data Management processes and their associated technology for:
  - project-specific initiatives
  - ongoing Data Management operations.

- Be prepared for unexpected off-cycle issues so that you can:
  - Keep high-priority projects going
  - Minimize the need to take money already allocated to projects.

- Ensure that everyone seeking funding knows how to proceed if they find themselves in an exceptional situation.

We're not talking about having a drawerful of templated business plans or canned arguments for why you need more money (although those aren't bad things to have on hand). Have a simple list of processes that need to be followed under different scenarios and know what to do in each scenario. These processes should address things like:

- How to distinguish the scenario into which you fall (funding classification process)
- Annual Budgeting process
- Off-cycle or emergency funding request process
- Funding prioritization process.

Some of these processes may be DM-specific, and some may be more global, with the most fundamental of these being, of course, your organization's annual budgeting process. Note that the mere exercise of establishing possible scenarios can point out situations you might overlook and where appropriate processes may be lacking.

I recommend creating a simple table like in Figure 24 to document your funding model. It's nice and concise and shows that although we may be looking for something comprehensive, it needn't be complicated. The example shown lists several possible funding scenarios.

The exact number of row and column headings can vary widely based on the nature and needs of your industry and even your specific company. For example, in addition to the scenarios shown in the example, you may have special approaches for:

- Initiatives that come from one or more Data Providers as opposed to one or more Data Consumers.

- AI or other advanced technologies that are treated distinctly from other initiatives.

- Regulatory initiatives that require a specific funding process.

- Internal initiatives may be funded differently from those that will be utilized by or directly impact parties outside the organization walls, such as customers, suppliers, business partners, and regulators.

Scope of Applicability	Annual Funding Cycle		Off-Cycle Funding	
	BAU	Project	BAU	Project
Enterprise	?	?	?	?
Region	?	?	?	?
Operating Unit	?	?	?	?
Domain	?	?	?	?

Figure 24: Funding Model sample template

Conversely, the buckets in the example may be more than you need. For example, you may or may not distinguish between BAU and project- or initiative-specific funding. Most companies have a general funding process that all parts of the organization follow. This would certainly address the process for Business as Usual (BAU) funding, but it may also address certain emergency scenarios as well.

The important thing here is *not* that Data Management invent elaborate new approaches to getting their money but that you ensure that there aren't any **types** of scenarios that will catch you off-guard. None of us could have predicted the huge impact of the COVID lockdown, but did your organization have an established approach for dealing with a natural disaster of that nature and magnitude? Were you surprised at the degree to which the extended lockdown became a Data Management issue?

Ask yourself if your standard annual budgeting process covers all eventualities. Do you have a Disaster Recovery Plan (DRP) or Business Continuity Plan (BCP) that addresses emergency funding measures? To the greatest degree possible, you want to anticipate the unexpected. It's not feasible to set aside cash for every eventuality, and sometimes changing priorities or outright emergencies mean you *do* have to "steal" money from Peter to pay Paul. Still, if your documented funding model addresses the scenario *in advance,* it helps people understand that *this is a possibility.* If Team A begins work on a project they know will be considered a low funding priority, perhaps they can build dependency contingencies into their project plans to minimize the "collateral damage" to related projects if Team A's project funding is cut or eliminated.

Remember that it's not a case of ensuring you'll have all the money you want in every scenario but rather that you don't waste time figuring out who you need to ask or what processes you have to follow to address funding in these scenarios.

Optional Sections

The preceding five sections are those that I consider most important in defining a Data Management Operating Model. There are, however, some other potentially valuable specifications that you may want to include. I'll address these in the remainder of this chapter.

Data Management Tool Stack

While I do not consider Data Management to be a technology function (even though it frequently sits inside the IT organization), it is undeniable that the DM organization requires a fair amount of software tooling to support its operations. The Technology Team must be involved in the tool selection process, and they may even be the ultimate arbiter of the choice of specific software solutions. This ensures interoperability as well as compatibility with the overall technology infrastructure. It is the task of Data Management/Data Governance to identify the *types* of tools they require and to lay out the specific functionality they need. It is this level of requirement that we expect to see documented within the Tool Stack portion of the Operating Model. These software tools will support the Data Management/Data Governance initiative in the various activities necessary to manage the Data Management Program in achieving trustworthy data, cataloging that data appropriately, and managing any Data or Data Management issues that interfere with achieving these goals. Depending on the level of maturity of your Data Management initiative, this outline may describe an already implemented tool stack or focus on the *requirements* for achieving your target state tool stack. In many cases, it will be a combination of the two.

In keeping with our Holistic Data Governance approach, do not define these tooling requirements in a vacuum. Factoring in the Strategic Goals and Strategic Actions that were defined in the Data Management Strategy, know what tools you need to support the operations that will lead to achieving those goals. Where appropriate, you can also include relevant use cases and interoperability requirements while working with the Technology team to identify appropriate solutions.

In addition to technical input from IT, you'll want to solicit requirements from all the key users (and potential key users) of your various tools to ensure the requirements fed to IT meet the needs of these users. Be sure that all such user requirements are *business-related functionality* requirements of these various user groups. Ensure that, collectively, you address the three main tool categories:

- The tools that the Office of Data Management needs to run the program. This can be very basic things like document repositories, budget trackers, and approval workflow engines.

- The tools to support fundamental processes such as Metadata Management, Analytics and Reporting, and Data Quality Management. These activities will demand tools like data catalogs, data quality engines, and various reporting tools (the latter may be quite extensive, depending on the complexity of your Analytics and AI programs).

- The tools to support the program's Governance activities (both Data Governance and Data Management Governance). Consider how you will manage requirements, data risks, issues, and the escalation and resolution of both program and data issues.

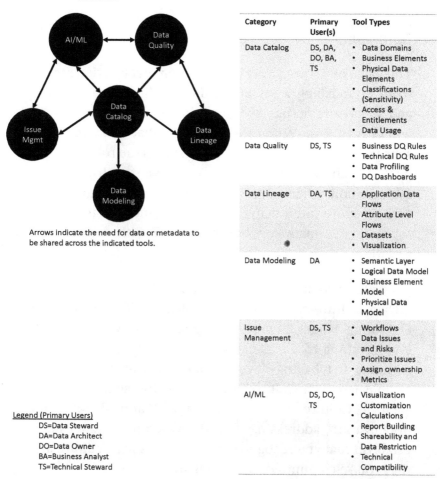

Arrows indicate the need for data or metadata to be shared across the indicated tools.

Legend (Primary Users)
DS=Data Steward
DA=Data Architect
DO=Data Owner
BA=Business Analyst
TS=Technical Steward

Category	Primary User(s)	Tool Types
Data Catalog	DS, DA, DO, BA, TS	• Data Domains • Business Elements • Physical Data Elements • Classifications (Sensitivity) • Access & Entitlements • Data Usage
Data Quality	DS, TS	• Business DQ Rules • Technical DQ Rules • Data Profiling • DQ Dashboards
Data Lineage	DA, TS	• Application Data Flows • Attribute Level Flows • Datasets • Visualization
Data Modeling	DA	• Semantic Layer • Logical Data Model • Business Element Model • Physical Data Model
Issue Management	DS, TS	• Workflows • Data Issues and Risks • Prioritize Issues • Assign ownership • Metrics
AI/ML	DS, DO, TS	• Visualization • Customization • Calculations • Report Building • Shareability and Data Restriction • Technical Compatibility

Figure 25: Data Management Tool Stack example

There are many ways to represent this in the Operating Model. It can be in the form of individual specifications for each tool type, a graphical depiction, a tabular listing, or some combination of all of these approaches. Figure 25 shows one such example.

Data Culture

The value of a strong Data Culture in an organization results from establishing a set of common beliefs, expectations, and behaviors across everyone in the organization who works with data. When we can *expect* that everyone has a sense of the *value* of data and understands the role that they play in achieving that value, we have the basis of an organization where everyone shares common goals and will, far more often than not, be highly inclined to react in a predictable manner when presented with various data situations.

It's still a fairly new concept to address the development of a Data Culture *construct* as part of the Data Management Operating Model, but I believe that it is a very forward-looking thing to do. There is no better expression of (or stimulus to) having "everyone on board" than a well-established Data Culture, and even if the achievement of such a Culture remains highly aspirational for your organization, addressing it in the Operating Model helps establish that you recognize the value of such a culture and that you're committed to building it.

When people share a common set of beliefs about data—when there's a significant degree of like-mindedness in the organization, that leads to:

- Improved Data Quality because people understand the downstream effect of errors and feel a responsibility to flag them.

- Easier Data Governance because people understand the importance of data being trustworthy.

- Greater innovation because more people are empowered to use data to make decisions and develop new ideas.

- Efficiency gains because people in different parts of the organization are working with a common language to achieve a common goal.

In short, such a degree of like-mindedness is at the core of making the whole organization your partner in Data Management.

Many of us are familiar with the concept of Corporate Culture. Viewed cynically, some may consider Corporate Culture to be just how greedy the business leaders are. However, when looked at in a more empowering way, Corporate Culture reflects the collective beliefs and behavior of ALL the people within the organization. Data Culture is simply that part of your overall Corporate Culture that addresses how people relate to data. So, if Corporate Culture is about:

- The values of the organization
- Beliefs about what is important
- Everyday actions and assumptions
- The way we do things around here

Then data culture can be said to be about everybody:

- Understanding
- Using and
- Looking after data
- As a normal way of working.

Put more simply, we begin to operate as if **data is integral to the way we do things around here.**

One way to define a Target State Data Culture is to catalog the *behaviors* we'd like to see present throughout the organization. For example, some behaviors that you'd expect to see in an established Data Culture are instances of people

- Understanding their role in the organization's data ecosystem

- Protecting and respecting data sensitivity

- Working collaboratively with other data users

- Understanding where "their" data is coming from and how to use it

- Highlighting data issues as soon as they spot them.

These behaviors are the things that we observe on the surface. But WHY do people exhibit (or *not* exhibit) these behaviors? In 1976, American anthropologist Edward T. Hall developed what has come to be known as the "Iceberg Model of Culture." No, it's not a description of how cold people can be in a modern society but rather of what drives us beneath the surface. You can find many variations of this picture on the internet, but take a look at the one in Figure 26.

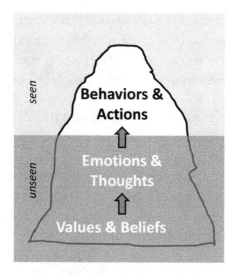

Figure 26: Iceberg Model of Culture

In Data Culture, as in most of life, our behaviors ultimately arise from our beliefs. How we behave around data reflects our beliefs about data in general and, very often, about data within our particular workplace. Our beliefs give rise to thoughts and emotions that lead to certain behaviors.

For example, we may like to think that we're professional and don't let our emotions impact our work. But is that really the case?

What if we believe that it's the responsibility of a particular group to ensure the accuracy of some set of data? Perhaps that's the Data Producer or maybe a central Data Quality team. In this paradigm, if we find errors in that data, it's human nature to be frustrated, maybe even slightly angry. We may not let emotions erupt in any obvious display of anger, but frustration and anger **will** influence how we behave. Maybe we decide, "The heck with them, I'll get the data somewhere else," or "We'll just build our own

DataMart with *accurate* versions of that data," or any of a dozen other possible behaviors. Notice as you read this if you actually consider one of those responses to be a perfectly "reasonable" response to such a shortcoming.

Now, ask yourself another question: What if your underlying beliefs were "wrong" (or at least "less-than-helpful") in the first place? What if there's a perfectly good reason why the data is consistently wrong, and what if that reason has nothing to do with the Data Provider?[32] There could be far more effective behaviors that would lead to a much more efficient environment.

Look back at our short list of "desirable behaviors" above. You'll see things like "work collaboratively with others" and "highlight data issues as soon as you spot them." These are every bit as reasonable as "The heck with them...", but they're also far more *constructive* responses. The problem is if your underlying beliefs are yelling things like "it's not my job," these alternate responses have little opportunity to assert themselves. Absent these more constructive thoughts, meaningful *behaviors* don't stand much of a chance!

The point of this little exercise is that if there are behaviors that you'd like to see, you need to give some thought to what sort of thoughts and emotions would drive those behaviors ("I should help to fix this," "I wonder what the problem could be?"). In turn, you need to think about what fundamental beliefs and values would give rise to those

---

[32] Maybe you're "piggy-backing" off of somebody else's feed (never a good idea, often formally prohibited by policy but we all know that it still happens) and the feed was actually built for specifications that don't match yours.

thoughts and emotions ("Quality is everybody's job," "What I say matters"). We're not talking about any kind of invasive assault on people's core personal, political, or religious beliefs. Still, we *do* want to feed some hopefully empowering information into people's beliefs *about data*!

Depending on the Corporate Culture in your organization, there will be a variety of appropriate ways to do this. When it comes to your Operating Model, you want to think about what types of learning, sharing, or influencing channels might lead to shifting people's beliefs about data and, especially, their relationship to data within your organization. You have many options for how to represent your target-state Data Culture in your Operating Model but, whatever visual style you adopt, you want to establish:

- WHAT behaviors you want to see
- HOW you might elicit those behaviors from people
- WHO you hope to influence.

Let's return to that earlier list of desirable behaviors and assess whether these are all specified at a level that allows us to tailor an "elicitation approach" to each behavior. Here's an edited version of that same list with a bit of normalization and some structure added in:

- Understand **the key roles** in the organization's data ecosystem:
  - o **Understand your role**
  - o **Understand the roles of those with whom you work.**
- ~~Protect and respect data sensitivity~~ **Understand your data:**

- o **Know what your data is *supposed to* look like**
- o **Know where your data is coming from**
- o **Respect the sensitivity classification of your data**
- o **Know the uses for which your data is suited.**
- Work collaboratively with other data users:
  - o **Know who to ask when you need assistance**
  - o **Know who to tell when you see a problem**
  - o **Share your insights with others.**
- ~~Understand where "their" data is coming from and what it can be used for (this is incorporated above).~~
- ~~Highlight data issues as soon as they spot them (this is incorporated above).~~

As we mentioned earlier with respect to our Data Structure (Figure 20), this list, although longer, is still not as comprehensive as what we'd expect to see in a real-life Operating Model. Still, let's see what it might look like to define some initiatives that could instill these behaviors. For illustration purposes, I've addressed some of these behaviors at the higher level (the outer level of bullets) and some more specifically (the inner level of sub-bullets). Take a look at Figure 27.

Don't worry about going too deep. You can build out further details when you begin to implement these initiatives. In addition to the WHAT/HOW/WHO we show in Figure 27, you could also address things like

- WHO will be accountable for the initiatives?
- WHAT sort of schedule will they be on?
- WHY is each of these behaviors important to you?

WHAT?	HOW?	WHO?
Understand each other's responsibilities	• Publish annotated org charts & role descriptions • Feature a staff member and their duties in company newsletter	Everyone
Understand what your data should look like	• Publish case studies about data quality (fit for purpose) • Regular talks by Data Owners about how they use their data • Create "why you want our data" mini-videos for internal web site	Data Providers Data Consumers
Respect the sensitivity of your data	• Training videos • Make it easy to find sensitivity classifications in a Data Catalog • Feature "pop-up quizzes" with recognition awards on internal web site	Data Providers Data Consumers
Know who to ask	• Publish annotated org charts • Publish data flows • Have team members describe how they see each other's role	Data Consumers Data Owners
Know who to tell	• Establish Data Sharing Agreements and SLA's • Publish annotated org charts and role descriptions	Data Providers Data Consumers QA Team
Share your insights	• Monthly subject-matter forums • Lunch-and-Learns • Offer recognition awards for innovative cross-team initiatives	Data Stewards SME's Data Producers

Figure 27: Data Culture definition example

Finally, don't hesitate to include some "all-encompassing" activities applicable to many of the desired behaviors. Hold little contests, design "learning games," have a weekly or monthly story-telling exercise. You may think that your organization is too "serious" to buy into this, but I've seen it work both at youth-oriented startup companies and at "stodgy old financial institutions." If not everyone wants to play, that's fine. Allow word-of-mouth to make the activities more popular. You won't establish a deep sense of data culture overnight, but your Operating Model should still reflect your longer-term vision of what you would like your Data Culture to look like.

Who's in the lead?

I once worked at a company where we made it a practice to end every meeting with a 5-minute online quiz. We took turns trying to come up with fun bits of trivia that were also intended to keep people thinking about our data culture. We included everybody, from senior executives to our most junior team members. We then created various levels of "competition." Did the managers get higher scores than the junior team? Did one office score better than the other offices? What individuals got the most right answers? Nominally, the only prize was bragging rights, but there were much bigger prizes insofar as we helped instill both our desired behaviors and an overall sense of camaraderie.

Program Metrics

William Edwards Demming[33] was famously misquoted (or, at least, quoted very much out of context) as saying, "You can't manage what you can't measure."[34] With all due respect to what Demming *actually* said, I'll assert that to manage your Data Management Program effectively, you need to be able to objectively measure your current state and your progress toward your target state. Well-defined metrics provide the "mile-markers" that keep you on course. Such mile markers are key to providing:

- A Standardized Reference Point that provides an objective baseline for determining where you are making progress and where you need to make progress.

- A Common Understanding as a result of consistently using the same metrics throughout the organization.

- Easier Resource Management as a result of knowing where resources are most needed.

---

[33] Never heard of William Edwards Deming? He was (amongst other things) an American economist and business theorist. After WWII, he was part of the American forces that helped rebuild Japanese industry. Based on what he saw, he helped develop the fundamentals of effective quality control, many of which are still in place today.

[34] Ironically for a quality control expert, this well-known quote is taken *so* out of context that it ends up being exactly the opposite of what he actually meant. The quote we usually get is, "If you can't measure it, you can't manage it." (what he *actually* said was, "**It is wrong to suppose that** if you can't measure it, you can't manage it." See https://deming.org/myth-if-you-cant-measure-it-you-cant-manage-it/.

- A basis for Celebrating Success because clear targets have been set and true "wins" can be identified.

I like to propose four types of metrics for assessing the overall progress of a Data Management Program:[35]

- Program metrics are measurements of how far you've gotten on your "to-do" list. Put another way, they tell you what you've accomplished so far.

- Outcome metrics address the "so what" factor...once you've accomplished a certain amount (as measured by the Program Metrics), how has that impacted your goals? More simply, what difference have your efforts made?

- Process metrics are similar to Outcome Metrics, but they focus on how effectively you're performing your Data Management activities. In other words, how efficiently are you getting to your goals?

- Financial metrics are any numbers that justify the existence of the DM program in bottom-line terms. Quite simply, what did it cost you to get to where you are and, by extension, was it worth it?

Depending on the specific metrics you define within each type, you may calculate these values weekly, monthly, quarterly, and/or annually.[36] Additionally, bear in mind

---

[35] These four types of metrics are taken from the EDM Council's Data Management Capability Assessment Model (DCAM). For more details on the intent of these different types of metrics, see https://edmcouncil.org/frameworks/dcam.

[36] On rare occasions, more frequent updating of the metrics may be of value, but unless you have already achieved a high degree of automation and can provide

that each of these types represents numerous specific metrics, many of which may be grouped together into *classes.* For example, if you were interested in measuring the successful establishment of your Data Governance Forum(s) (a form of Program Metric), you would probably want to assess the level of participation in the forum(s). Such participation, in practice, would probably be measured via an assemblage of numerous individual measurements, such as:

- Most Recent Forum Attendance
- Attendance as % Invited
- Month-to-Month Change
- Attendance by Role
- Number of Repeated Absences.

You could collectively refer to all these specific measurements as "Forum Participation Metrics." For our next two examples, we'll refer to this collection as the **class** of metrics within the **type**, "Program Metrics." [37]

Ultimately, it will be a combination of the Data Governance team, Senior Data Management managers, and various process owners who are responsible for ensuring that

---

one or more real-time dashboards, a sub-weekly frequency rarely provides additional value.

[37] For management purposes, some metrics may be prioritized via designations like Key Performance Indicators (KPI's) or Key Risk Indicators (KRI's). Although we define such designations in the Glossary at the end of this book, their designation is not relevant to the current discussion.

specific metrics are defined.[38] The Operating Model, however, guides the **types, classes,** and **frequency** of metrics we expect to develop. Because monitoring such metrics will drive the ongoing deployment of the Data Management target state, these metrics are very much a part of the various structures that our Operating Model should define.

Figure 28 illustrates one way to describe a structure for your critical metrics. Starting with the specific list of these **types,** optionally qualifying them with the **frequency** with which you expect to see them calculated, you would then list the various **classes** of metrics within each of those divisions.

Such a simple list of expected Metric Types, Classes, and (optionally) Frequency may be adequate for your particular needs. Figure 29 shows how we can provide further value by adding additional specifications showing

- Who is expected to produce each type (or class) of metrics (identify the roles that are accountable for the metrics rather than specific individuals).

- The primary audience for each of these **classes** of metrics. [39]

---

[38] As we will see in the next chapter, the Data Management standards are an appropriate vehicle for establishing many such specific metrics. Various process definitions (cf. Chapter 14) may also contain definitions of specific metrics.

[39] If your classes are too broad to be targeted at a particular audience, this "audience" specification may not be appropriate to your situation unless you can meaningfully redefine each class to be audience-specific. That much being

Always remember that you're not talking about *specific* metrics here but rather **types** and **classes** of metrics.

Figure 28: Program Metrics example

---

said, some metrics classes may legitimately be of very broad interest, potentially appealing to many audiences (or even to the entire organization). If this is the case, then by all means, call out the relevant audiences (not excluding the possibility of "Everyone") in your Metrics Class diagram.

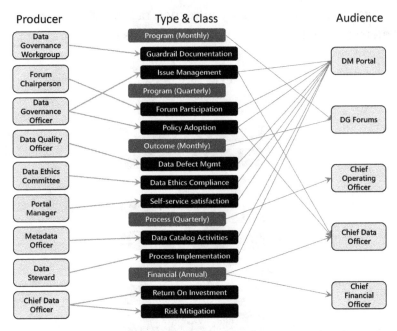

Figure 29: Program Metrics example with producer and audience

Finally, I'd like to emphasize once again that the Metrics Classes (the darkest boxes in Figure 29) do not represent any specific measurements. We expand on each box when defining specific reporting requirements, and each of these Classes would then contain a large number of actual metrics (see Figure 30).

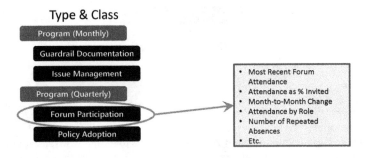

Figure 30: Class of metrics vs specific metrics

Category	Governance
Name	Operating Model
Description	How the Data Management function will be structured to meet the objectives of the DM Strategy.
What	**WHAT** WILL ENSURE THAT
Sample Level of Specificity	· "We will establish the following hierarchy of Data Governance bodies..." · "We will establish the following initiatives to grow our data culture..."
Characteristics	Structural approach, Prescriptive but at an organizational (rather than activity) level.

Table 5: Characteristics of Operating Model

TWELVE

Data Management Policy and Standards

Policy is how data will be managed to meet requirements. Standards are rules defining actions to comply with the Policy.

Although we'll explore Policy and Standards separately, let's begin by discussing them as a single, multi-level structure because these two work hand-in-glove even more so than the other document types in the hierarchy.

The Enterprise Data Management Policy is a high-level directive that expresses goals and represents management expectations for legal, regulatory, and organizational requirements. Put another way, it represents the core "set of rules" that will constrain and direct how business, technology, and operations will manage and control the data. As such, it is the primary guardrail document defining the mandatory practices needed to fulfill the goals of the Data Management Strategy.

A Single Policy vs Sets of Policies and Standards

Because many companies employ multiple Data Management Policies, I want to take a moment to underscore what I feel is the importance of having a single, enterprise-wide Data Management Policy. Such an overarching Policy ensures a constant approach to managing data throughout the organization and greatly facilitates the alignment of the DM Policy itself with any related mandates from other Control Functions.[40] It also helps clarify what mandates are most appropriately defined and enforced by Data Management instead of those that belong in the domain of other Control Functions, such as Privacy or Information Security. We will address this "unification of ideas" later in this chapter.

 Note that this is one of those "cases where you must be fully aware of what is demanded by your culture, standards or protocols." There may be one or more strictures in place in your organization that compel you to maintain multiple policies.

---

[40] As described in the "Related Control Function Guardrails" section of our Common Matter (see Chapter 4).

These could be little more than naming conventions (e.g., what we call "Standards" and "Guidelines" in this book may be called "Execution Policies" and "Guiding Policies" in your organization), or they could be as serious as a requirement that different activities are required to have distinct Policies controlling how they operate. The latter situation is especially likely if your Data Management function is not actually a sanctioned global control function but rather an aggregation of independent or quasi-independent groups (Data Architecture, Data Quality, Data Provisioning, etc.). To some extent, you can achieve the "One Policy to Rule Them All" structure by the simple expedient of having a "master" Data Management Policy[41] which is little more than an aggregation of links or references to all the "component" policies. The most important thing to remember conceptually is that, to the extent you can, the Policy or Policies should be straightforward and concise for the reasons laid out below.

Whereas the Enterprise Data Management Policy lays out the *types* of things that are deemed mandatory (e.g., "Metadata must be collected for all in-scope data."), a closely related set of Data Management Standards needs to be defined to provide specific, rule-based directives about how to comply with each of the mandates of the Data Management Policy (e.g., "This is HOW metadata will be collected."). Each standard comprises a set of rules defining expected actions for achieving compliance with the Enterprise Data Management Policy. To that end, the Data Governance function must drive the development of a Data Management Policy and associated Standards. These should

---

[41] Not to be confused with a "Master Data" Management Policy!

be written with input from all concerned business, technology, architecture, and operations stakeholder groups. Write them to control essential cross-organizational behavior while leaving room for operating unit-specific constraints.

Allow for OU-specific needs

In the early days of my career, I worked in the software development space, and I always hated being told what to do—especially by people who I felt didn't fully appreciate all the subtleties of my part of the business. Yes, I could be arrogant about that, but a decade or so later, when I started developing Enterprise policies and standards, I always took the approach that the Enterprise should clearly mandate everything that was necessary to fulfill on the broad, organization-wide goals but *no more*! Always remember to leave room for the individual Operating Units to manage their business-specific needs.

Dealing with Lagging Compliance

You should rigorously vet Policy and Standards to ensure that broad compliance is feasible, but you should not set the bar so high that you impose undue hardship on "lagging" parts of the organization. I'm not suggesting that you ignore important mandates, but rather that you consider adopting a "rising tide lifts all ships" approach. Consider how the more mature Operating Units can serve as models for (or possibly even as organizational mentors to) the less mature units. You can also write the policy that you "really want" but build in a tiered compliance schedule. Specify, for example, that practitioners must follow some parts of the Policy immediately upon publication, some parts within six months, and the most demanding parts within 12 months. This prepares the less mature operating units to plan for the long haul.

 Compliance is another case where you may run up against constraints on what you can say. Policies are typically subject to a high level of approval (often the Board of Directors), and some Boards may adopt a "zero-tolerance" approach to *any* "lagging compliance." You may be able to address this concern simply by adjusting the "tiered compliance schedule" to be a single compliance date that gives adequate time for full compliance with all mandates. Another approach is to take the most demanding mandates out of the policy (if legal or regulatory drivers do not prohibit doing so) and, perhaps, publish them as interim guidelines (see Chapter 15).

The number of options that may or may not be open to you should make it clear that whoever is writing, vetting, and approving the Data Management Policy (basically, all DM/DG leaders) needs to have a thorough understanding of the organization's protocols for enforcing policies. It will come as no surprise that I consider the enforcement of these particular guardrail documents (Policy and Standards) to be one of the most important defensive activities of the Data Governance organization. Whatever you arrive at for compliance with your Data Management Policy, it should be spelled out clearly in the Compliance section of your Common Matter.

Common Matter

In Chapter 5, we discussed the various types of Common Matter to include in most of your guardrail documents. While we found that some sections of the Common Matter may have limited relevance to the "higher-level" guardrails, *all* of the Common Matter is highly relevant to both Policy and Standards. Figure 31 recaps the Common Matter for us.

Rationale
Provides the underlying reasons and justifications for establishing the document, highlighting its significance to the organization, its intended audience, and its relationship to the other governance guardrails.

Scope & Applicability
Specifies the data, processes, and activities subject to the policy's coverage and the operating units or roles impacted.

Compliance
Outlines expectations for demonstrating adherence to the guardrail's mandates, mechanisms for overseeing such adherence, and processes for managing exceptions and escalations.

Related Control Function Policies
References other policies, standards, or procedures that intersect with or enhance the effectiveness of the current document—demonstrates integration and alignment with broader organizational controls.

Accountability
Identifies the owner of the document or document section and their specific responsibilities for maintaining and managing it.

Publish & Approval Log
Records version history, publication dates, and approvals related to the document—provides a clear historical record of changes and endorsements, fostering transparency and accountability.

Glossary
Defines any acronyms, technical terms or potentially ambiguous terms used in the document. These should be avoided in general but, where necessary, define them in the Glossary.

Figure 31: Guardrail "Common Matter" recap

Policy Mandates

After assembling the Common Matter, we proceed to the main portion of the Policy—that is, all the specific mandates that constitute the "meat" of the document. I recommend stating these mandates in the format:

"In order to _____ you must _____"

This is not meant to be an inflexible template. The "in order to" phrase may be a *list* of goals, "you must" may actually refer to a specific role (e.g., "...the data steward must..."), and the final phrase, like the "in order to" phrase, may list a closely related set of steps. The important thing to remember is that the overall statement should provide us with a high degree of unambiguous instruction on what is expected of the practitioners.

Each statement should be:

- High-level and principle-based
- Absolute and unambiguous.
- Concise but Comprehensive

Viewed in aggregate, the statements should further:

- Cover all the specific needs of your organization.
- Be supported by detailed specifications in the form of Data Management Standards.
- Ideally, leverage accepted Data Management Standards in your industry and, if applicable, address compliance with relevant regulatory mandates.

I want to underscore the bullet: "High-level and **principle-based**." Earlier, we talked about defining Principles of Data Management, how these Principles can inform our Business Objectives and, more fundamentally, how they feed into establishing our Strategic Actions. We want our Policy Mandates to align with those Strategic Actions, but since the Actions themselves are, in part, a response to our Principles, we also want to ensure that we account for these Principles in our Mandates. In short, the Mandates should constrain our behavior such that we align with:

- The Principles by which we operate.
- The Strategic Goals that we have set for ourselves.
- The Strategic Actions we have defined for achieving those Strategic Goals.

This was expressed diagrammatically in Figure 14 and is shown in a broader context in Appendix B.

The use of the phrase "you must" (or alternatively, "<this role> must") in these statements is very intentional. For the first time in our Guardrail Hierarchy, we are now seeing very specifically stated and fully enforceable mandates. Phrases like "you should" or even "it is necessary that" are ambiguous in their meaning.

The intent of Policy statements is to make clear that some specific set of individuals (most often identified in terms of their assigned roles) has an obligation to do something. If you say something like "The Data Steward *should*..." you are making a recommendation. Using emphatic language like "The Data Steward *must*..." removes the optionality of a recommendation and turns the statement into a requirement.[42]

Why does this Matter?

This sort of "justification-enabled" approach to stating your Policy mandates helps:

- Ensure efficient approval, adoption, and compliance.
- Minimize the need for frequent revisions.
- Eliminate redundancy and possible contradictions across mandates.

There are additional advantages to keeping your Policy concise, but this may be more clearly seen by comparing the "Compact" policies that we are discussing here to bulkier, nominally more comprehensive policies. I'll refer to this latter approach of more detailed Policies as "old-style" and the more Compact approach as "new-style."

Detailed Policies vs Compact Policies

A concise format for policies represents a fairly recent trend in Data Management/Data Governance circles (hence my calling them "new-style"). Historically, it was

---

[42] We'll revisit this distinction between "should" and "must" in Chapter 15.

not uncommon for policies to be quite lengthy, often providing extensive, in-depth information on:

- The background of the policy (and, perhaps, of an organization's approach to Data Management in general).

- Equally detailed justification for the creation of the policy, usually going far beyond what we'd expect to see in our Common Matter "Rationale" sections. In some industries, the justification was often the imposition of some kind of penalties by a regulatory or other oversight body, and I have seen Policy introductions that gave detailed descriptions of such regulatory citations.

- The reasoning, methodology, and/or rationale for how the policy was crafted.

- Detailed descriptions of every single mandate, including who is required to perform what specific actions in order to ensure compliance.

This was not done for purely "Proustian" reasons (i.e. because the policy's author(s) felt the need to share their infinite wisdom in a correspondingly epic degree of detail!), but rather because there was a thought that an Enterprise Data Management Policy should be:

- The authoritative reference for all things related to Data Management.

- The sole repository for this important information (i.e., everything in one place).

- A master reference with the power to address any Data Management issues that might possibly arise.

This wasn't the only reason that policies became bloated... sometimes they *did* start out small, but due to a lack of proper governance, they accreted more and more mandates, stipulations and justifications, growing over time into unmanageable and sometimes self-contradictory tomes that created as many problems as they addressed!

In all but the smallest organizations, any guardrail document classified as a "policy" typically has a rigorous vetting, approval, and publication cycle. In many organizations, the approval process alone requires several levels of sign-off–often with one or more requisite C-suite signatures and possibly even the imprimatur of the Board of Directors. As such, you don't want to update your policy any more frequently than a prudent review cycle would demand (typically annually).

It is obvious that the weight of such an onerous process is not at all well-suited to maintaining a document that contains a wealth of detail. When an event as trivial as a change of responsibilities could require an update (and subsequent re-approval) of the entire Policy, we are willfully jumping into a sea of red tape.

In recent years, an increasing number of organizations have taken a streamlined approach to policy documentation. These "new-style" policies provide concise, high-level documentation of (at most):

- Some important context.

- Terse, high-level mandates (with details left to tightly coupled standards).

- Language around compliance and enforcement (as addressed in our "Common Matter" above).

- Reference to related guardrail documents (whether other Data Governance Guardrails as discussed in this book or to data-related guardrail documents from other Control Functions).

These shorter documents are every bit as much an authoritative reference as was the "old-style" policy document, but this more compact form minimizes the need to update, re-approve, and re-publish the document. Their focus on high-level, principle-driven mandates means it takes a significant change of Strategic Goal or a completely new Business Objective to force an update to the Policy.

In short, it makes the Policy more resilient and stable over time. Further, such a concise approach is a major contributing factor in creating a tightly integrated hierarchy of guardrails that keeps greater levels of detail in the more execution-related parts of the guardrail hierarchy (such as standards, processes, and procedures).

If anyone thinks that having a single policy (as I recommended at the top of this chapter) is incompatible with this "keep it concise but comprehensive" approach, I can only say, "Quite the contrary!" It may take some effort, but by having a complete set of well-constructed, compact mandates in our recommended "In order to..." format, you can create a short Policy document that covers all your mandates.

The "new-style" approach has a further benefit when overseeing policy compliance and adjudicating compliance violations and requests for exceptions to the Policy mandates. When the Policy is dense, detailed, and cumbersome, any such "matters for review" require escalation to a higher governance body (refer back to the section on Governance Structure in Chapter 11).

When escalating any matter, you want to be able to present the associated issue(s) clearly and concisely. Executive or board-level review committees do not want to receive pages and pages of minutiae. A concisely written Policy may not eliminate the need for a deeper examination of isolated issues, but it does minimize the need.

Issue Escalation with a "new-style" Policy can often involve a two or three-paragraph summary (including a citation of the relevant part of the Policy) rather than pages and pages of cross-referenced justification, intent, constraints, and the like. Additionally, it typically means that, whereas "old-style" exception adjudication might require technical, architectural, and business representatives to jointly present a case, the "new-style" approach means a single knowledgeable representative (such as a Data Steward) can often present the concern clearly and concisely. This reduces crowding at the executive level and streamlines the process by sending someone who knows how to converse with an executive committee to meet with that committee.

Keep It Simple!

I once worked with a large, multi-national bank whose Data Management Policy was over 200 pages long. It was so laden with cross-references and exceptions that the Data Governance group had a person whose full-time job was to ensure that the Policy was internally consistent and aligned with the other Control Function policies. Even so, when I reviewed their materials, I found cases where one section of the DM Policy said that "Activity X.Y is the sole responsibility of the Data Steward" and then, 20 or so pages further along, I read that "Activity X.Y is the sole responsibility of the Data Owner." The risk of such inconsistencies is always high with a complex, "old-style" policy.

The "new-style" approach that I espouse here makes it much easier for even a casual reviewer to spot these contradictions before they are inadvertently approved and enacted as "law."

So what *are* the actual "In order to _____, you must _____" statements that belong in your policy? Let's return to the fundamental tenet of this book–that your guardrail documents should form a tightly linked, holistic hierarchy.

As such, the Business Objectives inform the Strategic Goals & Actions of our Strategy. The Strategy drives both the structures we define in our Operating Model and, in turn, the mandates of our Policy. That means there's no "right answer" to what your Policy needs to address other than that, in aggregate, it must mandate a consistent approach to fulfilling the Strategic Goals and performing the Strategic Actions defined in the Data Management Strategy. That much said, here are some typical statements you might find in a Data Management Policy:

- *In order to* ensure our most valuable data is maximally cared for, *each Data Steward must* prioritize data, identifying all data elements central to our business operations.

- *In order to* ensure everyone's responsibilities are clearly understood and that DM functions are properly executed, *the Office of Data Management must* prepare detailed descriptions of required Data Management roles and their associated responsibilities and accountabilities.

- *In order to* ensure data accountability remains within the business process where data management is most effectively executed, *the process and data created by the process must* have common ownership – ownership must be assigned to the person with authority to effect process and data change.

- *In order* to ensure shared data has a common source of record and is managed consistently, *each Data Steward must* establish approved Systems of Record and Provisioning Points with assigned Data Owners and Data Stewards.

- *In order to* ensure data is widely, clearly, and unambiguously understood across the organization, *each Data Owner must* develop, approve, and maintain business definitions and associated metadata for all Critical Data Elements in a commonly accessible repository.

The specific statements you create will be driven by what you deem necessary to fulfill the goals of your DM Strategy (factoring in industry standards and, if relevant, any regulatory mandates). The examples above may be too high level for you. Remember that the "in order to...you must..." format is a pattern, not a rigid formula. In particular, you may want to add some clarifying language or deviate slightly from the pattern in the interest of the readability of a specific mandate. I've intentionally created some variety in these example statements to illustrate this kind of "deviations-from-the-format" without abandoning the pattern. At least in the initial draft, it's useful to stick to this format when developing your Policy statements. Regardless of the degree to which you do or don't follow the pattern, *follow the **intent** of the pattern* and, above all, keep the statements simple. Don't get bogged down in details, and don't try to cram multiple mandates into a single statement. As we're about to see, the Policy is not the place to get into the nitty-gritty of what mandatory compliance looks like on the front lines.

So, if the Policy does not spell out details of approach or execution methodologies, where **does** that language belong? Let's address that by first looking at how a "new-style" policy relates to the Data Management Standards in the hierarchy.

Relationship of Standards to Policy

Looking at Figure 32, we see three key characteristics:

- The Body of the Policy (i.e. the content after the Common Matter) consists of a set of terse statements in the form "In order to [achieve X], [role] must [do Y]."

- Each of these statements (or, perhaps, each *group* of closely related statements) will correspond to a single Data Management Standard.

- Each of these Standards will be expressed as a series of rule-based controls with associated monitoring metrics.

The list of statements in Figure 32 represents what many organizations want to address, but they are not intended as any kind of authoritative or even recommended list. As discussed above, we write Standards in support of specific mandates in the Policy, and these mandates relate directly to specific goals as spelled out in the DM Strategy (which, in turn, were developed to support the achievement of the organization's Business Objectives). As such, there's no one *"right"* list of Standards to have. What is important is that you let your priorities cascade down through the Holistic Hierarchy.

Your Standards should have a direct relationship to your Policy statements. Once again, you want to practice thinking of your guardrails as a Holistic Hierarchy, with the primary goal being to manage data in a way that directly supports the achievement of your Business Objectives.

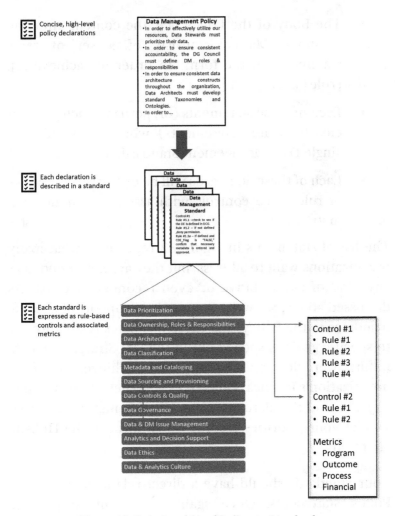

Figure 32: Relationship of Policy to Standards

What Does Standards Content Look Like?

Any given Standard will consist of one or more controls that define the intended outcome of that Standard (and hence ensure compliance with the corresponding mandate in the Policy). We express each control as one or more rules, which, ideally, can be automated. Associated metrics help define criteria for successfully implementing the indicated Standard or control. Let's arbitrarily drill down into one of the proposed Standards from our previous example and see what it might (in part) look like.

In practice, your Metadata Standard will probably have quite a few very specific controls around the identification, vetting, creation, and ongoing governance of your metadata. For illustration purposes, let's look at a single, multi-rule control and some possible associated metrics (again, your real-world example would probably have quite a few additional metrics associated with even this one example control).

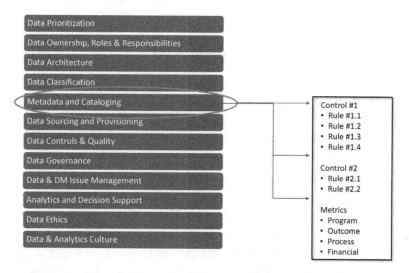

Figure 33: Data Management Standards - drilldown

To begin with, what do we mean by "controls" and "rules" in this context? Let's start with a definition of a *data control*. While different practitioners may have job-specific notions of specific *types* of data controls, for our purposes, we can define a *data control* simply as "a set of rules that direct, mandate, or constrain some kind of data-related activity." Thus, for example, a data quality rule, executed at a certain point in the data provisioning pipeline or at a point in the data life cycle would be a very simple data control.

While we often think of that type of control as an automated function, a control need not be automated (although we adopt this "made-up-of-rules" construct specifically to facilitate the automation of the controls).

The control we'll look at (to which you could assign a name or simply a number within the Standard) ensures that we cannot create a physical data element in any data store until we define, approve, and post a minimal set of associated metadata to a centralized Enterprise Data Catalog.

As we'll see in the next chapter, these control definitions can begin to look very much like process definitions. For now, let's just say that the difference is primarily a question of specificity. A rules-based control within a Standard focuses more on the activity to perform rather than on the system or infrastructure-specific steps that constitute a process or procedure definition.[43]

In the Introduction to this book, we discussed the growing need for automation in any data ecosystem of even modest complexity. Notice that although the rules shown in Figure 34 *can* be followed by a person, they are all specified in language that, given the appropriate support software (whether home-grown or third-party), can easily be

---

[43] We will discuss this distinction further in the next chapter.

automated. Not all your controls will be amenable to automation. Some are inherently "people" controls–either because of the nature of the Standard or because some kind of human judgment is required.

For example, one of the holy grails of business glossaries for many years has been the automatic definition of business data elements and even business terms. While generative AI, especially with carefully governed language models, can finally produce useable output in this area, such definitions still require a certain amount of human oversight (even if crowd-sourced) to ensure that the definitions are accurate, unambiguous, and complete.

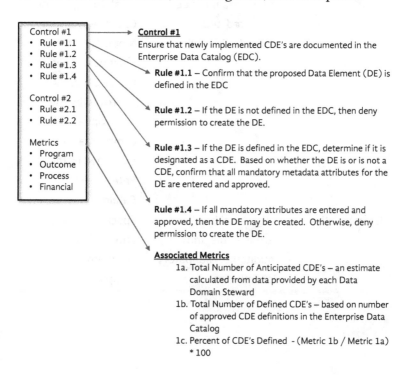

Figure 34: Rules-based Data Management Standard example

Category	Governance	Governance
Name	DM Policy	DM Standard
Description	High-level directive that constrains how data will be managed to meet legal, regulatory and organizational requirements.	A rule or set of rules that defines infrastructure-independent actions for achieving compliance with the DM Policy.
What	**WHAT** WILL ENSURE THAT	**WHAT** WILL ACCOMPLISH THAT
Sample Level of Specificity	"Comprehensive Metadata must be collected and published for all CDE's."	"Within 15 days of establishing any new CDE, the following Metadata attributes must be defined for the CDE (...), approved by the <appropriate committee> and published to the Enterprise Data Catalog."
Characteristics	High-level but enforceable and auditable. Mandatory compliance.	Specific, enforceable and auditable. Mandatory compliance.

Table 6: Characteristics of Policy and Standards

THIRTEEN

Execution Guardrails

We have now reached a point in the Holistic Data Governance Guardrail Hierarchy where we are controlling fairly specific activities. Our Vision, Principles, and Objectives have led to Strategic Goals and Actions that demand a certain set of operating structures. We have seen how carefully defined rules-based controls in our Standards can facilitate compliance with a set of precise Policy mandates. However, we are not quite at the "hands-on" level yet. To wrap up our traversal of the Holistic Data Governance Guardrail Hierarchy, the next three chapters will examine how we control and manage the execution of our day-to-day activities.

We will incorporate carefully documented *Processes* and *Procedures* that provide step-by-step instructions that tell us not simply *what* to do but *how* to do those things in a specific environment. Such standardized specifications ensure consistency, repeatability, and ease of training/knowledge transfer.

In a use of the term that may be at odds with how you've heard it in the past, we define *Guidelines* to be advice and suggestions that do not *mandate* specific behaviors but that clarify potentially vague situations, define best practices, or offer guidance on what to expect in terms of future mandates.

And finally, the very unsexy, old-fashioned *Roadmaps* and *Project Plans* rise up to say, "I'm not dead yet." They may have been around for a long time, but these two document types, often ignored as part of the DM/DG control framework, are still valuable documents that help us control what we expect to see accomplished in the short- to mid-term.

Figure 35: Execution Guardrails

Notice that the "WHAT will accomplish that" arrow is carried down from our Governance Guardrails (see Chapter 10). This is yet another example of "Connective Tissue" across the various document types. As the *Data Management Standards* defined the types of activities that we must execute to comply with the mandates of the *Data Management Policy*, so the *Processes* and *Procedures* define the environment-specific steps that operationalize those activity types.

FOURTEEN

Data Management Processes and Procedures

A Process is a series of steps to take to achieve a desired outcome. A Procedure is a low-level task within a Process that specifies how to perform an activity.

For those of you who are excited to start writing very specific, step-by-step guardrails, here's your chance to shine! Processes and Procedures both involve documenting how we do things. Processes are highly specific, step-by-step instructions for performing an outcome-producing activity *in your environment*. They not only address each required step but also adapt those steps to the forms, tools, and other environment-specific things that need to be utilized while performing the activity. Additionally, they may provide context-specific alternatives, incorporating flowchart-like branching logic (e.g., "If the result is X, do Y, otherwise do Z").

Procedures are, in effect, "sub-processes." Much like subroutines in a computer programming language, they are self-contained series of steps that describe how to perform some kind of "sub-activity" that may occur multiple times in a single process or that may recur across multiple processes. For example, your customer onboarding process might include some kind of simple activity, such as confirming identity, which is repeated at different points during the larger onboarding process. Documenting it as a procedure not only allows for more compact documentation but, more importantly, ensures consistency across the larger process and, indeed, across a larger body of processes.[44]

Processes and Procedures must be clearly defined across all aspects of the Data Management and Data Governance activities, such as:

- Data Governance
- Issue Management
- Architectural Considerations
- Data Quality Management
- Cross-Control Function Collaboration

---

[44] Some organizations use "Process" and "Procedure" to define very distinct types of activity, but in this book, we will align with the EDM Council's definitions as just described (and as defined in the Glossary at the end of this book).

Consistent enforcement of documented processes and procedures ensures consistent execution methodology and precise repeatability, even when accountable process experts move on to new positions.

As we saw with our documentation of Data Management Standards in the previous chapter, the inclusion of metrics (process-related metrics in this case) within your process documentation allows for continuous monitoring of the effectiveness of the processes and can identify where improvements are needed.

In keeping with the specific nature of process documentation, we usually look to the individual Process Owners to provide comprehensive documentation of each of their processes. To ensure effective knowledge transfer when staff changes, the documentation must be clear, unambiguous, and readily accessible to everyone involved in the execution of the process.

While there is value (especially vis-à-vis assisting knowledge transfer) in documenting even the most localized processes, the standardization of those processes that are executed regularly across multiple Operating Units will deliver the greatest consistency benefits.

Why do Process Definitions Matter?

"The Way Things Work Around Here" or "This is How WE Do It" are not just slogans of the "not invented here" apologists. Consistency of execution provides efficiencies of scale, predictable results, and simplified training. All too often, even while acknowledging these values, process owners rely on "tribal knowledge" amongst a small number of process experts who "just know" how to perform a certain process. Documenting this knowledge in a clear, unambiguous, and standard manner is neither trivial nor (for most people) fun. Even those of us who started our careers as programmers often lack the discipline to ensure we capture every nuance of a business process. You can't rush this step. If your organization has been operating for any significant period of time, especially without any major disruptions,[45] it will be a major effort simply to identify all your significant data-related processes, much less to rigorously document them. However, once a critical mass of processes is documented, the standardization of these processes:

- Leads to consistency of results.

- Facilitates continuous process improvement (you can't assess, much less improve, the efficiency of a process that is not executed in a consistent manner).

---

[45] The extended COVID lockdown that started in March of 2020 is not often viewed as a Data Management or Data Governance event and yet the literal overnight need for much of our staff to work remotely presented huge challenges to technical, data, and business staff throughout almost all industries (industries whose presence was primarily online (such as social media sites) were far less disrupted by the event but even they were largely caught unawares by the sheer magnitude of the shift in focus). I consider it not at all coincidental that the busiest years of my Data Management consulting career started in March 2020. The huge disruption was a giant wake-up call to many companies. The smartest of them quickly embraced the disruption as an opportunity to take a very serious look (for some, their FIRST serious look) at how well (if at all) they manage their data.

- Minimizes re-training when a new person moves into a role.

- Retains knowledge when "that one person" leaves the organization.

- Supports defensibility of compliance to your auditors (whether internal or external).

Given this list, especially the bullets about knowledge retention and transfer, the criteria for prioritization may not be immediately intuitive. Processing a sale is, obviously, a business process of very high importance. It literally defines your income stream. However, that process may already have a large degree of "pseudo-documentation" (or at least "pseudo-standardization") insofar as much of it is probably implemented in software. It *is* important to document that process (even for completely automated online order processing, documentation of the processes facilitates future software updates).

However, depending on the nature of your business, you may want to move your emphasis to the more human-centric processes. This is especially true for processes related to positions with high turnover (such as helpdesk or customer support). It's not that these processes are inherently more critical to running the business but rather that standardization will provide a more immediate "bang-for-the-buck."[46]

---

[46] Think back to the comparison of value vs. criticality we made when discussing the prioritization of our Strategic Goals and Actions in Chapter 9. We are talking about a similar kind of prioritization of process documentation here.

Nobody likes to document but...

Having spent the early years of my professional career as a programmer and then as a manager of programmers, I can assure you that many programmers will insist that "the code is the most accurate documentation you can have." While there is a kernel of truth in that assertion, it completely disregards the fact that few people can make sense of that particular form of "documentation." I have literally seen instances of programmers returning to their own code months after they initially wrote it and scratching their heads in puzzlement over what they intended in some part of a module. While the parallel of documenting a business process and writing a computer program is not a perfect analogy, neither are the two completely dissimilar.

What is the Best Way to Document a Process?

The only real answer to this is "in detail." Depending on your culture, business, or even the specific process, you want to choose a documentation approach that makes the process definitions comprehensive and easy-to-consume. Broadly speaking, in most organizations where I've worked, processes are documented in one of two formats: outline or diagrammatic/graphical.

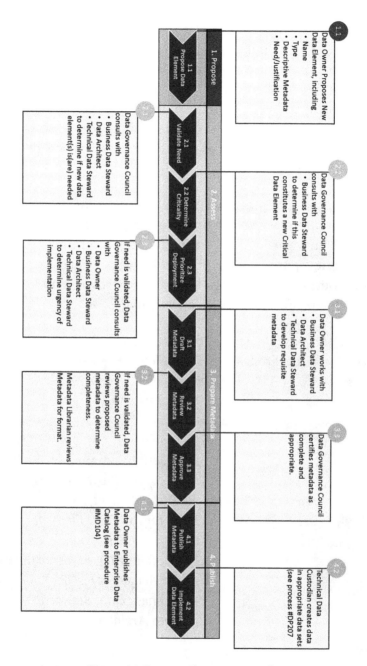

Figure 36: Process diagram example

Figure 36 is a graphical representation of a process for defining the metadata for a proposed new data element prior to implementing that element within one or more data stores.[47] Note that this diagram can be quickly referenced at a very high level but it also includes call-out boxes that provide additional details on performing each step (including references to other processes and control documents).

If you have a more formalized culture or if you are documenting a more complicated process, an outline format may make this material more consumable. For illustration purposes, here is the identical process defined as an outline (which, you'll note, also provides additional "real estate" for more detailed wording):

1. *Propose the Data Element*
   1. *Propose the Data Element*
      1. *Data Owner Proposes New Data Element, including*
         1. *Name*
         2. *Type*
         3. *Descriptive Metadata*
         4. *Need/Justification*
2. *Assess the Need for the Data Element*
   1. *Validate the Need for the Data Element*
      1. *Data Governance Council consults with the following to determine if new data element(s) is(are) needed.*
         1. *Business Data Steward*
         2. *Data Architect*

---

[47] This is closely related to the example we gave when illustrating Rules-based Controls in the previous chapter.

3. *Technical Data Steward*

2. *Determine if the Data Element is a Critical Data Element*

    1. *The Data Governance Council consults with the Business Data Steward to determine if this constitutes a new Critical Data Element*

3. *Prioritize Deployment of the Data Element*

    1. *If the need is validated, the Data Governance Council consults with the following to determine the urgency of implementation.*

        1. *Data Owner*

        2. *Business Data Steward*

        3. *Data Architect*

        4. *Technical Data Steward*

3. *Prepare the Associated Metadata for the Data Element*

    1. *Draft the Metadata describing this Data Element*

        1. *The Data Owner works with the following to develop requisite metadata*

            1. *Business Data Steward*

            2. *Data Architect*

            3. *Technical Data Steward*

    2. *Review the Metadata*

        1. *If the need is validated, the Data Governance Council reviews proposed metadata to determine completeness.*

    2. *The Metadata Librarian reviews the Metadata for format.*

  3. *Approve the Metadata*

    1. *The Data Governance Council certifies metadata as complete and appropriate.*

4. *Publish the Data Element*

  1. *Publish the Metadata for the Data Element to the Data Catalog*

    1. *The Data Owner publishes the Metadata to the Enterprise Data Catalog (see process #MD104)*

  2. *Implement the Data Element in all Requisite Data Stores*

    1. *The Technical Data Custodian creates the data in the appropriate data sets (see procedure #DP207)*

Why do I Need Procedures on Top of All That?

To be precise, you *might* need procedures **under** all that (or at least some of it). As discussed earlier in this chapter, a certain series of steps may need to be executed repeatedly in different processes or at different points within a single process. Put another way, it's a bit like a subroutine or function definition in programming (and, indeed, you may even want to define your procedures in a quasi "input parameter" fashion so that you can leverage the same definition in different situations). Our process definition above ends with step 4.2, "Implement Data Element." The call-out box says, "Technical Data Custodian creates data in appropriate data sets (see procedure #DP207)."

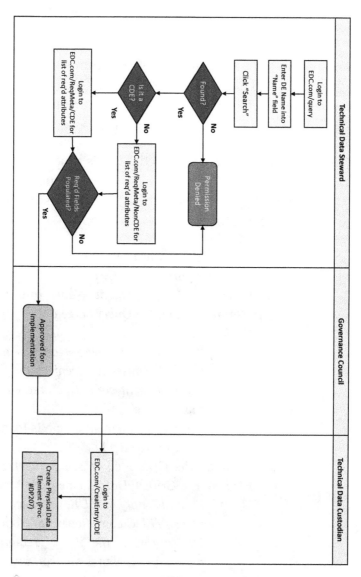

Figure 37: Procedure flow example

Figure 37 shows what that hypothetical DP207 might look like in a graphical format (in this case, we use a more traditional flow-chart type of diagram with the addition of "swim lanes" for additional clarity).

Note not only the high degree of environment-specific references but also that one of the "steps" ("Create Physical Data Element") is actually itself a procedure. Yes, procedures can contain other procedures.

And, again, here is the same Procedure, this time in a text-based outline format (which, as we discussed in conjunction with Figure 36, can provide the "real estate" for more detailed instructions):

I.   *Technical Data Steward confirms suitability*
   a.   *Connect to https://EDC.com/query*
   b.   *Enter the Data Element Name into the "Name" field on the Query Screen*
   c.   *Click "Search"*
      i.   *If the Data Element Name is not found, Permission is Denied, and the Data Element cannot be created at this time*
      ii. *If the Data Element Name Is found, continue to step I.d.*
   d.   *Examine the CDE Flag to see if the Data Element is a Critical Data Element*
      i.   *If it is not a CDE, connect to https://EDC.com/ReqMeta/NonC DE to review the list of required metadata attributes and continue to step 1.e*
      ii. *If it is a CDE, connect to https://EDC.com/ReqMeta/CDE*

> *to review the list of required metadata attributes and continue to step 1.e*
>
> e. *Confirm that all the required metadata attributes have approved definitions for this Data Element.*
>> i. *If not all fields have approved definitions, Permission is Denied, and the Data Element cannot be created at this time*
>> ii. *If all fields have approved definitions, continue to Step II.*
>
> II. *The Data Governance Council automatically approves the Data Element for creation.*
> III. *Technical Data Custodian creates the Physical Data Element*
>> a. *Connect to https://EDC.com/CreateEntry/CDE*
>> b. *Refer to Procedure #DP207 to Create the Physical Data Element.*

Note that, on the surface, this procedure is very similar to our control example from our discussion of DM Standards in Chapter 12. It's the degree of infrastructure-related specificity that makes this example a procedure and our earlier example a Standard. Whereas our Standard spelled out specific things to accomplish, it did so in a manner that is applicable to a variety of infrastructure environments. This is necessary because the same Standard may need to be followed by Operating Units with varying operating environments. By contrast, the Process and Procedure definitions are "cookbooks" that direct you, where appropriate, to distinct data stores, systems, and applications and tell you what "buttons to push" once there.

Finally, I'd like to point out that the similarities between this Procedure and the earlier control illustrate how straightforward it is to turn a rules-based Standard into one or more specific Processes/Procedures. I've added swim lanes to this example, and these declare that much of this procedure contains manual activities. Still, you can also see that, given the appropriate software tools, we can easily automate these steps.

Of course, not all business processes are so readily mechanized, but where resources permit automation, it is useful to have process definitions that are readily adaptable to such automation.

Category	Execution
Name	Process and Procedures
Description	· A series of steps that, when executed in order, achieves a desired outcome. · A low-level step or task in a process that specifies how to perform an activity.
What	**WHAT** WILL ACCOMPLISH THAT
Sample Level of Specificity	"To create a new entry in the Enterprise Data Catalog, perform the following steps..."
Characteristics	Highly specific, enforceable and auditable. Infrastructure-specific. Mandatory compliance within stated scope and applicability.

Table 7: Characteristics of Processes and Procedures

FIFTEEN

Guidelines

Recommended best practices.

Of all the guardrail types defined in the Holistic Guardrail Hierarchy, "Guideline" is the one that seems to be used in the most varied manner by different organizations. I know Data Governance Officers who insist that a Guideline is an enforceable mandate and I've seen long lists of process-specific "Guidelines" embedded within (mandatory) standards documents.

I'm going to follow the EDM Council's definition of "Guideline" here and say that a Guideline is:

A recommended best practice that
1. *Supports implementation of a standard or interpretation of policy requirements; or*

2. Addresses areas not covered by existing policy documents.

For our purposes, Guidelines are suggestions–they are not enforceable mandates. They are "good ideas" or "best practices" that may not be relevant to all Operating Units. While we can use them to clarify parts of a Policy or Standard that may seem ambiguous or incomplete in isolated situations, they are, more fundamentally, a way to impart knowledge of industry standards and best practices while acknowledging that some parts of the organization may not be ready to "raise the bar" that high. In this sense, we can use them to drive maturity across the organization without making unrealistic demands on all Operating Units.[48]

Although optional, many parts of the organization may have an interest in proposing them. The Data Governance group should, of course, vet these to avoid the proliferation of too many well-intentioned but ultimately superfluous "recommendations", but I call this out simply to highlight that, unlike many of the other Guardrail Documents, there is no one group that should be tasked with drafting them. They may originate in business, architecture, technology, or operations groups.

Guidelines can be very broad in nature (e.g., "You *should* check Data Quality whenever data moves from system to system.") or they can be specific to a particular process (e.g., "You *should* include the Technical Data Steward whenever you develop metadata for a Critical Data

---

[48] As mentioned back in Chapter 12, Guidelines can also be useful in situations where "tiered compliance schedules" are not permissible.

Element."). Notice the use of the word "should" in these sentences. Any given guideline *could* be a mandate within a Process, Standard, or Policy. The key factor is whether we word it as a suggestion or as something people "must" do.

Guidelines may not be a critical component of the Holistic Data Governance Guardrail Hierarchy but neither are they simple "icing on the cake." In particular, Guidelines that provide advice on topics not easily controlled by mandates (such as How to Craft a Meaningful Business Definition for a CDE) can add significant value to your overall Hierarchy.

Some examples of different types of guidelines are:

- **Support for an existing standard** – Protection of Personal Information (PI) is not just a fundamental concern of [our company], it is also a legal requirement. Some information not identified as PI may, in fact, be leveraged by "bad actors" to create associations across multiple datasets to make nominally anonymized data identifiable as belonging to an individual. If there is any suspected risk of this being the case when developing a new data extract (whether in conjunction with application development or as an informational extract), it is strongly recommended that the involved parties consult with representatives from the Analytics team to assess the degree of risk involved with this particular data and with the Legal team to determine any potential legal exposure.

- **Interpretation of a standard** – When deciding whether to designate a Data Element (DE) as a

Critical Data Element (CDE), the Data Owner should consider:

- o Whether or not the DE plays a role in a Business Process designated as a Critical Business Process.
- o Whether said process requires that the DE be guaranteed to be the most current view of the data for the process to function correctly.
- o Whether the process requires an elevated degree (>99.9%) of accuracy to function correctly.
- o Whether out-of-date or inaccurate values of the data would cause the process to be assigned an elevated Risk Rating (as defined by the organization's Data Risk Evaluation Matrix).

- **Recommendation for a specific scenario or functional team** – Whenever video is processed by the "Image Tagging" tool, pay special attention to video originating from the Visitor Screening desk. Although the "Image Tagging" tool is intended to identify and conceal any personal information included in videos, these videos should be manually "spot-checked" on a regular basis to ensure that presented identification (such as Driver's Licenses) are not readable in the video.[49]

- **"Raise the bar"**—Whenever we can automate the discovery and documentation of data lineage for a

---

[49] NOTE: This is a prime example of a recommended guideline which might be elevated to a formal mandate if it is found that the referenced "Image Tagging" tool is not performing adequately.

particular set of Data Elements (DEs), we should document the lineage for those DEs in a level of detail that shows both the movement and any transformations of the DE at each "hop" along its corresponding Data Supply Chain.[50]

If some of these seem like they *should* be mandates in your organization, remember that no Guideline is inherently a recommendation or a mandate. Any Guideline recommendation can be turned into part of a mandatory guardrail simply by changing the word "should" to "must." This is not meant to be a semantic game. We call out Guidelines as a distinct type of guardrail specifically because:

- General advice is sometimes more helpful than a hard-and-fast rule.

- It is not unusual for different Operating Units to be at different levels of maturity, and a recommendation that lets people know what is possible is more motivating than a command to do something that is impossible (or, at least, highly onerous) within their current state environment.

---

[50] NOTE: This sort of Guideline clearly assumes that the default Data Lineage mandates in the company are less stringent than "every hop" documentation...perhaps because the existing process involves significant manual intervention. The default, for example, may be to document Data Lineage only when the Data Element moves from system to system or, perhaps, from one Operating Unit's environment to that of another.

Category	Execution
Name	Guidelines
Description	Recommended best practices that: 1) support implementation of a standard or interpretation of policy requirements; or 2) address areas not covered by existing policy documents.
What	**HOW** WE'D LIKE YOU TO DO THAT
Sample Level of Specificity	"Before entering any metadata into the Data Catalog, you should solicit input from the Data Owner, the Business Data Steward, the Data Architect, the Technical Data Steward and any relevant Subject Matter Experts."
Characteristics	General in nature but may be specific to one or more activities. Recommended but not required. ***Not enforceable.***

Table 8: Characteristics of Guidelines

Sixteen

Roadmaps and Project Plans

> *A Roadmap is a high-level schedule of implementation expectations. A Project Plan is an ordered list of specific steps for implementing a capability.*

A Roadmap defines what you want to achieve over a mid-term timeframe and how to allocate resources across the component initiatives effectively. In short, it provides a high-level schedule of when we expect to implement various capabilities. There is no one "right" timeframe for an effective roadmap. Depending on how clear your overall target state vision is, how interdependent your various milestones are, and how secure you are in ongoing resource availability, your roadmap may cover a few months or a few years. My experience has shown that

Data Management Roadmaps are most meaningful and effective as guardrail documents when covering a one-to-two-year timeframe. This is a sufficiently long period to allow for a comprehensive vision without being so long that vagaries of future resource availability can cast doubt on the viability of the vision.

As we discuss in more detail below, Roadmaps can define the rollout of business capabilities (i.e., functionality) or of the infrastructure implementation necessary to achieve that functionality. There is an obvious synergy there, and I recommend developing functional and related infrastructure roadmaps in tandem.

Project Plans are, of course, a well-recognized tool in almost any workplace, Data Management/Data Governance organizations no less so. A Project Plan provides a detailed list of the tasks that go into fulfilling a single goal (or, perhaps, a closely related *set* of goals). It spells out detailed task breakdowns, the amount of work entailed in each task, cross-task dependencies, and role-based (sometimes people-based) resource assignments.

Roadmaps and Project Plans are seldom classified as Data Governance guardrail documents. Still, they are an important part of the Holistic Data Governance Guardrail Hierarchy insofar as they plot the direction that the Data Management Program will take over time. Used in conjunction with a comprehensive set of metrics, they enable you to weave an objective narrative that states where you've been, determines where you want to go, and keeps track of how close you are to getting there. They also help you identify trends and link these to your costs—to know if your efforts are paying their way in results.

Roadmaps and Project Plans are rarely leveraged to create such a narrative, but I think that's a lost opportunity. In addition to describing where we are on our implementation journey, they are highly effective tools for involving all of your stakeholders. You'll be asking a lot of them (both individually and collectively) as you expand your Data Management initiative, so make sure they know that their efforts are appreciated and acknowledge the specific ways you recognize them as valuable to that expansion.

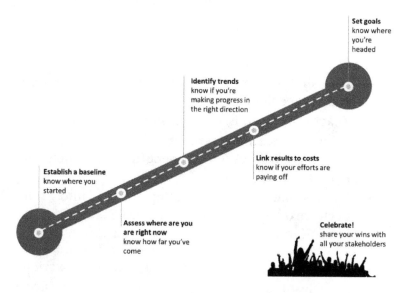

Figure 38: What a Roadmap can tell us

As mentioned earlier, Roadmaps (and Project Plans) are, in fact, tactical in nature. Parts of your Roadmap(s) will tie only indirectly to your specific Strategic Goals, but if you've been designing and implementing your guardrails *Holistically*, by the time you get to Roadmaps, they will, at least to a large degree, represent the tactical plan for implementing your Strategy.

Every methodology comes with its own approach to documenting Roadmaps and Project Plans. You'll have to look at the specific requirements of your organization (factoring in your industry standards and, if relevant, any regulatory mandates) to ensure you address any relevant protocols but, fundamentally, there are three levels of specificity:

Business, Functional, or Capability Roadmaps lay out the business functionality you plan to implement (we often refer to such functionality as Capability). This will include things like:

- Establish Data Governance Council
- Publish Enterprise Data Management Policy and Supporting Standards
- Enact Integrated Issue Management Process
- Adopt standard taxonomies and methodologies for the classification of all secure data (including Personal Information)
- Incorporate Policy Compliance into the Performance Reviews of all Data Management Executives.

Note that these are not task-based goals but, rather, various levels of Milestone. Unlike a "point-in-time" milestone marker on a traditional Project Plan, each capability on a Capability Roadmap will indicate the estimated time to *achieve* that capability milestone. You may also assign accountability for such achievement to one or more roles or groups. Additionally, these achievements may have dependencies. Looking at our list of examples above, we can see that you cannot "Incorporate Policy Compliance into Performance Reviews" until you have published the

Policy and Standards with which we must comply (see Figure 39.A).

Any of these functional goals may be fairly simple or may require multiple coordinated projects to implement. It may take time to "Establish Data Governance Council." Still, the overall capability is a fairly "monadic" milestone involving a limited number of steps (even though some of those steps might be time-consuming). "Publish Enterprise Data Management Policy and Supporting Standards," by contrast, will (as we'll discuss next) imply multiple, parallel workstreams to (at a minimum) "Define the Policy" and "Define [each of] the supporting Standards."

If it seems at times that the level of specificity may be arbitrary, remember to think in terms of the specific capabilities you define and choose a level that represents a genuine functional capability. Identifying the membership of a Data Governance Council does not provide any meaningful functionality, but having those people meet regularly in accordance with an officially approved charter *does* provide meaningful functionality. You need the former to get to the latter, but it is the latter that represents the target functionality.

Project Roadmaps summarize distinct projects or execution initiatives. As implied above, these projects may be one-to-one with the capabilities of our Functional Roadmap, or there may be some degree of decomposition. For example, establishing our Data Governance Council will likely involve a series of relatively sequential steps:

- Draft Terms of Engagement for the Council
- Define the responsibilities of members

- Assign members
- Seek enforcement authority from the Board of Directors
- Begin Meeting.

Publishing our Policy and Standards, by contrast, will have distinct workstreams with (most likely) different accountable parties and so might involve a series of projects like:

- Prepare Policy
- Prepare New Standards
- "Retrofit" Existing Standards.

Given our Holistic Guardrail Hierarchy concept, with its tightly coupled Policy and Standards construct, it would be necessary to, at minimum, draft the individual mandates of the Policy before even being able to identify the requisite supporting Standards. Again, the level of specificity may seem somewhat arbitrary, but a key rule of thumb is to define projects with an eye on the degree to which they can be managed and executed independently of one another. Pay particular attention to the degree to which you need the same resources for potentially parallel workstreams. If you cannot provide adequate resources, you may have to define a milestone project as a single project with internal sequencing rather than to roadmap these as distinct projects. Note that this does not mean that the Project Roadmap cannot express simple cross-project dependencies (as with our Policy and Standards example above), but intricate cross-dependencies probably indicate projects you can combine into a single deliverable.

Again, indicate approximate durations on the Project Roadmap. You may also wish to identify the groups or individuals ultimately responsible for delivering each project (see Figure 39.B).

Project Plans will be familiar to most readers of this book, and I will not provide any commentary on how most effectively to manage or even how to document a Project Plan. The choice of a Work Breakdown Schedule, Gantt Chart, Timeline, or Task Sequencing view and whether you leverage a Waterfall, Agile, Lean, or Kanban methodology is a decision for your Project Managers or perhaps your Project Management Office (if you have one). I will only say that each of the individual boxes on your Project Roadmap should translate into a single Project Plan. Break down the broad, milestone-like goals of the Roadmap into constituent tasks. High-level responsible parties from the Roadmap will be expanded into specifically accountable resources (specified as either roles or individuals), Roadmap durations will become specific start and end dates (perhaps additionally distinguishing between elapsed duration and work effort[51]), and so forth (see Figure 39.C).

---

[51] This distinction is all too often ignored, even by experienced Project Managers. Some tasks are inherently time-constrained. A one-hour meeting will take one hour, and you cannot make it faster by assigning more people to attend (if anything, that is likely to have the *opposite* effect!). Most tasks, however, may take more or less elapsed time than the actual effort involved. For example, if you estimate it will take four weeks to document a set of processes, you can reduce the duration by assigning additional people to create the documentation (assuming they are equally adept at the task). Conversely, if there is a single executive who must review and approve a document but that executive is only available for two hours a day, this will stretch what is nominally a four-hour review task over two days of duration.

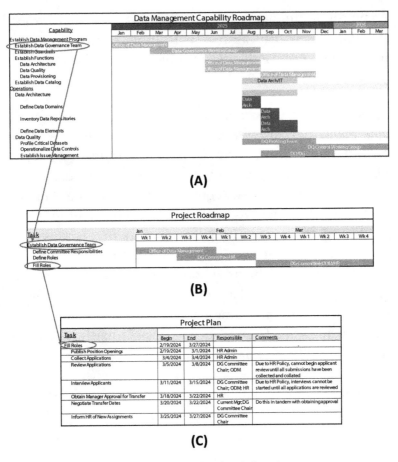

(A)

(B)

(C)

Figure 39: Three levels of planning

Whereas Data Management/Data Governance may regularly review progress against your Capability or Project Roadmaps and perhaps even use this as a basis for reporting to their management, they are less likely to focus on individual Project Plans unless they happen to have some specific responsibility or accountability in one or more of the Plans. Still, we include Project Plans in the Holistic Guardrail Hierarchy because they are the supporting detail for execution against our Roadmaps and can be a useful reference for diagnosing missed targets on a Roadmap.

Figure 39 shows examples of each type of document. These are much briefer than any actual roadmap or project plan would be in practice, but they illustrate the primary features that we highlight here. Note that the three types of planning document represent a mini-hierarchy of and in themselves with:

- Capability Roadmap – a strategic map of the functionality we plan to implement
  - o Project Roadmap – a high-level tactical map of what we will do to implement that functionality
    - ▪ Project Plan – a detailed drill-down into a specific deliverable from our tactical map.

Category	Execution	Execution
Name	Roadmap	Project Plan
Description	A high-level schedule of when various capabilities are expected to be implemented.	Specific step-by-step instructions for implementing a specific capability. The plan should show assigned resources, expected start and end times, allocated funding and appropriate oversight.
What	**WHEN** WE'LL DO IT	**WHEN** WE'LL DO IT
Sample Level of Specificity	N/A	N/A

Table 9: Characteristics of Roadmaps and Project Plans.

SEVENTEEN

Some General Advice

I'd like to close with a few words about how to get the people in your organization excited about adopting the Holistic Data Governance Guardrail Hierarchy. One of the most important ways to lay the foundation for this is to involve your stakeholders at the earliest levels of design. Let all your stakeholder groups have a seat at the table and ensure that you have representation from the various business groups, technology groups, architecture,[52] and data governance. Depending on the nature of the particular guardrail document you are developing, elicit input from Internal Audit to ensure that your specifications are clear and unambiguous. Also, consider involving someone from your Legal team to see if you are exposing yourself to any kind of legal risk in the document (as Consumer Data Protection becomes an increasingly common legal mandate, this legal input becomes increasingly relevant to

---

[52] If your organization happens to have distinct Business Architecture, Data Architecture, Information Architecture and Technology Architecture teams, all should be invited to the table.

the Data Management team). Don't neglect any groups that may have special requirements[53] for data, such as Human Resources or Vendor Management.

As you craft the individual documents, be clear about *why* you are writing each particular guardrail. Where relevant, tie particular documents (or even particular mandates within a document) back to the organization's pain points so that people are clear that the command to "Do X" is not an arbitrary imposition of authority. It is designed to address a problem that is widely recognized *as* a problem. The "Rationale" section of the Common Matter is a prime place to do this, but in the case of the Policy, you can also leverage the "In order to..." statements to indicate that a specific mandate is designed to address a particular issue or concern that is prevalent in the organization.

We have spoken about metrics at a number of different levels of the Guardrail Hierarchy. As you begin to roll out your guardrails, leverage these metrics to document your results. Broadcast your wins both far and wide. Actively seek out, publicize, and celebrate the places where guardrail compliance has produced:

- improved time to market
- faster issue resolution
- reduced data defects
- more effective business insights

---

[53] Of particular concern would be the need for special privacy (or other sensitivity) classifications and/or particularly stringent constraints on usage of their data.

or any other things that are meaningful to your various audiences.

It is also important that you consider the *consumability* of your document–how easy is it for your stakeholders to make sense out of all the guardrails you've worked so hard to create?

Begin by considering the overall **User experience**. Is the text semantically accessible? Put more simply, are your guardrails *easy to read*? These documents are not your invitation to write the next Great American Novel. The language can (in fact, *should*) be precise and perhaps even technical, but *clarity* is equally important. If you can say something in fewer words, do so!

Don't stop at clarity, however. Also ensure the *consistency* of the document. Have you checked for conflicting information? Defining the responsibilities and accountabilities of individual roles is an area where I most frequently see discrepancies across (and even within) documents. Have you made it clear *who* needs to do *what*?

It shouldn't need to be said, but it is critical that you make your Guardrails readily available. I have seen far too many companies put their Strategy on one SharePoint site, their Policy on some other document portal, the Standards get spread across multiple locations, and Process definitions end up on the laptop(s) of one or more individuals. Well-meaning aggregation attempts can sometimes be even more confusing if they aren't carefully thought out. Your specific organizational needs may vary, but, in general, I recommend that you make the effort to establish a single Holistic Data Governance Guardrail Portal that is the

System of Record[54] for all your guardrail documents. Work with the appropriate document owners and the technology group to ensure the portal truly works (see "The best laid plans..." callout below). Guardrail documents rarely require high-security classifications within the walls of the organization. Still, ensure that any such constraints that may exist are well understood, making it easy for interested parties to access this portal.

The best laid plans...

I once worked with a client that had created a "master index" site with links to all their guardrail documents. Unfortunately, it was done in a way where updates to the documents were not detected, and links to deleted documents just broke. Further, just because you had permission to access the master index did not mean you necessarily had permission to access the underlying documents. It was a great idea, but with nobody seeking the input of all involved parties, the execution was significantly flawed and created more frustration than convenience for the people trying to use it.

When we discussed Common Matter, we discussed the importance of documenting references to guardrail documents from elsewhere in the organization (i.e., from Control Functions other than Data Management/Data Governance). If possible, make it easy to get to *those* documents as well (e.g., don't just *list* them in your

---

54 AKA, the Golden Source, the Source of Truth, the Master Copy—in short, the authoritative source for the documents.

Common Matter, *link* to them). Your stakeholders should always be clear about how any particular document fits into the larger scheme of guardrail documents across the organization.

Particularly in our discussion of Guidelines, we mentioned the importance of not making unrealistic demands across the organization. Part of making your documents *consumable* is to make them *applicable*. Raise the bar, by all means, but recognize that you may need to raise it in increments. Ensure that your guardrails empower the Data Management organization rather than terrify them.

I've already mentioned giving Internal Audit a seat at the table when creating your guardrails. Whether you do that or not, review the final drafts with them. One of an auditor's "super-powers" is to assess the precision of a specification. You want to ensure that your documents pass the "auditability test." That is, is the language sufficiently clear that an auditor who is not an expert in some process area can read your guardrail document and objectively assess whether or not an individual or group is complying with that guardrail?

Finally, we mentioned the importance of broadcasting your wins. You must develop objective measures to *identify* those wins but consider how to broadcast them. Different audiences will be interested in different results and different levels of specificity about those results. Develop appropriate communication channels to share your wins with a wide variety of audiences. Perhaps your Data Governance team wants detailed, real-time dashboards, while a broader audience might be better served by a monthly newsletter. Your Board of Directors will want to see Financial and Risk-reduction metrics while your Data Quality team will be more interested in defect resolution efficiency. In enacting your Data Governance Guardrail Hierarchy, you've probably asked a lot from stakeholders across the entire organization. Whether they participated willingly or not, they deserve to know that it was worth the effort–that it was worth *their* effort (willing or not!).

Be generous with your praise, acknowledge individual contributions and you're very likely to see much less reluctance to participate in future Data Governance endeavors.

Conclusion

We must have a coherent, integrated approach to structuring our guardrail documents to establish effective control over a complex data and data management landscape. We can summarize our **Holistic Data Governance Guardrail Hierarchy** as follows:

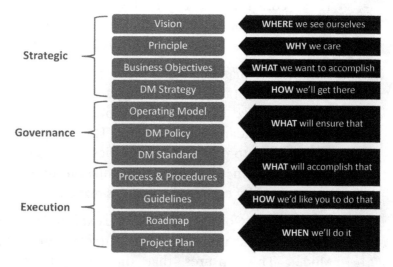

Figure 40: Summary of Guardrail document types

As we move from the very broadly focused Vision Statement to the most specific Project Plans, there is a "connective tissue" that links each document, minimally, to the one beneath it and, frequently, to other guardrails in the hierarchy. These relationships appear in detail in Appendix B, but let's summarize a few of the most important relationships:

- The Business Objectives drive the Strategic Goals. This is perhaps the single most meaningful correlation in the entire hierarchy because it is the point at which the Data Management initiative declares how it will support the overall business in achieving success (as defined in those Business Objectives).

- The Strategic Goals and the associated Strategic Actions drive the mandates laid out in the Policy. These constrain the day-to-day operations of all Data Management practitioners in a way that will help ensure that the Strategic Goals are achieved.

- The Policy mandates drive the individual Data Management Standards. We implement each broad, principle-based mandate in the Policy by way of a series of Standards-specific rules. This allows for a stable, easy-to-communicate Policy with details spelled out in ways most meaningful to those constrained by each of the Policy's mandates.

- The Strategic Goals and Actions are executed within the various structures defined in the Operating Model. This ensures that the organization is constructed to provide the most efficient and relevant support to achieving those Strategic Goals (and, in turn, the overall Business Objectives).

In the Introduction to this book, we compared Data Governance Guardrails to the protective barriers that help keep you safe on a twisting, winding mountain road. You expect to see those guardrails installed consistently and to have an associated supporting structure (such as road signs that warn you of particularly risky conditions lurking around the bend). The barriers can't prevent every single accident (there will always be some people who either put too much faith in them and, conversely, there will be those that think the warning signs don't apply to them because "I know what I'm doing.") Likewise, the most intricately integrated guardrail hierarchy in the world will not *guarantee* the success of your Data Management initiative but, like the protective roadside railing, it will help keep the majority of people moving safely and efficiently on their journey.

There's no **one right way** to define your Data Governance Guardrails, but there is a coherent, integrated approach to building out a set of Guardrail documents that work *as a whole*. Documents that reinforce one another with common themes focus on achieving **Holistic Data Governance**–an approach to Data Governance that respects the localized needs of the individual parts of your organization while orchestrating them into a meaningful whole that helps deliver the data that your organization needs at all levels to make meaningful decisions about how to succeed in your particular industry.

About the Author

 David Kowalski, Ph.D., has spent his entire professional life showing organizations how best to manage and govern their data. David is the Founder and Principal Advisor at MIDAS Advisory Services, an executive advisory firm based in Princeton, NJ, that focuses on providing guidance to senior Data Management and Data Governance leaders. He has worked with executives at large and mid-sized corporations around the world to assess their Data Management practices and help devise strategies and policies to improve their efficiency, effectiveness, and reliability while mitigating risk exposure. An industry thought leader, David appears regularly at conferences across the United States and is a very active contributing member of the Enterprise Data Management Council, where he plays a leadership role in guiding the ongoing development of the Data Management Capability Assessment Model (DCAM).

With four decades of both hands-on and managerial experience in Data Management, David began working on the software development side before switching his focus to the business aspects of Data Management and Data Governance. This experience has convinced him that if the fundamentals of your approach are not firmly established, all the fancy technology in the world will only give you more garbage at an ever-increasing rate of speed.

When David is not writing or talking about Data Governance, you'll likely find him hiking up a mountain somewhere or else spending time at home with his wife, his ever-expanding library and a not-quite-as-quickly-but-also-expanding clowder of rescue cats!

You can contact David at
david.kowalski@midasadvisory.com.

Acknowledgments

No man is an island and no book is truly the work of a single individual. There may be one author name on the cover of this book, but it would be disingenuous to claim that I did it by myself. I could not have done this without the help and support of a number of other people.

I have to begin by thanking the inimitable Gwen Thomas. Gwen and I had been crossing paths on the conference circuit for many years before we actually started sitting down and having one-on-one conversations. We quickly became friends, and when we were saying goodbye at the end of the Data Governance and Information Quality (DGIQ) Conference in June 2024, she casually said, "Your presentation was very interesting...have you published it?" Within five minutes, she had very diplomatically defused all of my excuses as to *why* I had not published it (most of which were as original as "I don't have time" and "I don't wanna") and convinced me that I had no valid excuses for not expanding that material into a book. Her deep knowledge of Data Governance, of the history of our industry and, coincidentally, of the publishing business made her an invaluable reviewer of the content and a font of wisdom about how to most effectively present my ideas. Thank you, Gwen. This would have been a far less effective effort without your input (OK, let's be honest: it would have been a non-existent effort without your input!).

Thanks to my friends and long-ago bosses, Ted Hills and John Bottega, who, many years ago in very different ways, helped finalize my transition from the technical to the business side of Data Management and helped me to start playing on a much bigger stage.

To my former colleagues Mark McQueen, Cindy Sullivan and Matt McQueen, the countless number of "yeah, but...", "what if..." and "how about..." discussions we had over the years provided me (and, I hope, them!) with a much stronger and more nuanced understanding of the Data Management/Data Governance space.

Thanks to the EDM Council for permission to incorporate several of the definitions from their online Business Glossary into the Glossary in this book. I have been personally involved in developing much of the content in the Council's Glossary and, along with the EDM Council management, I would like to see these definitions adopted as cross-industry standards for Data Management practitioners.

To Tony Shaw and all the wonderful staff at Dataversity: It's been well over a decade since I first met you, and you still keep inviting me back to speak at the Enterprise Data World (EDW) and Data Governance and Information Quality (DGIQ) conferences, where I have met so many wonderful people from all walks of the Data Governance/Data Management space. Without the vast range of perspectives I've encountered at these events, I don't think I could have formulated the ideas that comprise this book.

I first met Data Governance/Data Management Consultant Matthias Vercauteren at those same EDW & DGIQ events, and we rapidly became friends (if you have the chance to meet Matthias, I expect you'll immediately agree with me that it's very hard **not** to rapidly become friends with him!). Matthias introduced me to Steve Hoberman of Technics Publications, and if it was Gwen who provided me with the motivation to put pen to paper in this effort, Matthias was very instrumental in my finding an outlet for the final product!

And that leads us to Steve Hoberman himself. Thanks for believing in this book, Steve, and for being such a wonderful partner in bringing it to market!

Saving the most important acknowledgment for last, my undying thanks and love to my wife, Lonna, who had to endure far more than my usual degree of babbling every time she asked, "How's the book going?" Much of this babbling, she assures me, sounded like "blah, blah, blah, Data Governance, blah, blah, blah" to her, and I can only hope that it doesn't sound that way to my readers! Since I'm the cook in the house, she also had to hear an awful lot of "Sorry, honey, I don't have time to make dinner tonight," but at least we got to go out for dinner far more than usual!

Glossary

Business Objective – a result or target that business planners or executives intend to achieve within a stated time. *Business Objectives* can be defined at the Enterprise or Business Unit level.

Business Unit - the customer-facing parts of the business that offer distinct types of services to those customers. Also known as *Lines of Business*.

Capability - a defined and demonstrated ability to accomplish a specific task or set of tasks in a repeatable fashion.

Capability Model – see *Data Management Capability Model*.

Centralized Data Management - an approach to Data Management in which concepts and standards are defined and, very often, executed by a central authority.

Control – see *Data Control*.

Control Function - **A function within an organization that is accountable for some dimension of controls that apply across all areas of the organization.** Control Functions are often a second *Line of Defense*. Responsibility for the implementation of controls resides with business units and functions. The control function defines the requirements of the controls, assists with their implementation, and verifies their ongoing operation. (*) Note that some companies refer to these as "Shared Services" rather than "Control Functions". As discussed in the body of the text, Data Management (and Data Governance) is a Control Function, but many of the other Control Functions in the organization will also have something to say about what to do with data. Information Security and Privacy are very obvious instances, but Finance and Legal may also have policies that impact how data is managed and even HR may have a surprising amount to say here.

Critical Business Element - **A business element that is deemed materially important to one or more business processes.** The criticality is a business process requirement and thus is assigned to the business element. A data element is not critical unless it is designated as a component of a critical business element. Risk associated with this business element can be categorized based on adverse impact without adequate controls. Criticality is proposed by either the business that produces the data in their business process or by a consumer of the data. Criticality is approved as part of the data governance process. Per enterprise data management policy, the critical designation results in requirements for escalated data quality controls and recorded evidence in the metadata for both the business and data elements. Some organizations use "critical" and "key" as synonyms of each other, while other organizations view "critical" data elements as a higher priority than "key" data elements. (*)

Critical Data Class – a high-level specification of Data (such as a Data Domain) that is identified as being of essential strategic or tactical importance to the operation of the Business.

Critical Data Element - **A data element that is aligned to a critical business element and is deemed materially important.** The criticality is a requirement of the business process and thus is assigned to the business element. A data element is not critical unless it is designated as a component of a critical business element. Risk associated with this business element can be categorized based on adverse impact without adequate controls. Criticality is proposed by either the business that produces the data in their business process or by a consumer of the data. Criticality is approved as part of the data governance process. Per Enterprise Data Management Policy, the "critical" designation results in requirements for escalated data quality controls and recorded evidence in the metadata for both the business element and the data element. Some organizations use "critical" and "key" as synonyms of each other, while other organizations view "critical" data elements as a higher priority than "key" data elements. (*)

Current State – A summary snapshot of all capabilities that are currently implemented within your Data Governance/Data Management organization.

Data Asset - **A data asset is any collection of data owned by an organization that is considered to have intrinsic value.** Examples include, but are not limited to Document, Database, Electronic medium, Video, Audio, and Website form. (*)

Data Control - a set of rules that direct, mandate, or constrain some kind of data-related activity.

Data Domain - see *Logical Data Domain.*

Data Governance (Function) (DG) - **The function that defines and implements the standards, controls, and best practices of the data management initiative in alignment with strategy.** Data governance is responsible for creating and implementing a data control environment. According to the Basel Committee on Banking Supervision (BCBS) – a data control environment consists of a set of policies governing all aspects of data acquisition, distribution, integration, and usage that are sanctioned by executive management, based on standards, implemented across the data lifecycle, with clear accountability and monitored by audit. The function includes, but is not limited to:

- Designing and implementing the framework (including associated processes) necessary to sustain a data control environment
- Establishing the operating model required to achieve governance objectives
- Defining and implementing policy, standards, and operating procedures
- Establishing and implementing the data accountability mechanisms
- Developing and implementing metrics needed to monitor and report on data management progress
- Designing and implementing data governance training programs (*)

Data Management (DM) - The development, execution, and supervision of plans, policies, programs, and practices that deliver control and protection and enhance the value of data and information assets throughout their lifecycles. (*)

Data Management Capability Model - a framework that defines a set of *Capabilities* necessary to support the implementation of a comprehensive Data Management practice.

Data Management Program (DMP) - an organizational function dedicated to managing data as an asset throughout an organization. (*)

Data Management Strategy (DMS) – A statement of approach and prioritization for how the Data Management function will support the achievement of the Business Objectives.

Data Risk - The potential for a loss related to your data. The risk could be through a wide range of risk categories, such as regulatory risk, compliance risk, reputational risk, data breach, and data loss. (*)

Data Risk Appetite – The degree to which an organization is willing to accept some level of Data Risk in the expectation that it will increase the chances of some kind of "reward" or payback.

Data Risk Appetite Statement – A formal articulation of an organization's *Data Risk Appetite.* In practice, this would usually be a section of a more general Risk Appetite Statement.

Data Risk Management – The development, execution, and supervision of plans, policies, programs and practices that deliver control over an organization's *Data Risk* exposure. Such control typically extends to the definition, identification, assessment and, where appropriate, mitigation and remediation of such risk. Data Risk Management is normally part of a broader Risk Management function.

Data Strategy – While this term is sometimes used as a synonym for "Data Management Strategy (DMS)," we use it to designate a specific *component* of the DMS. Specifically, the Data Strategy is the portion of the DMS that addresses the Data Content that is key to achieving our strategic goals and the types of approaches we will take to leveraging that data (i.e., the strategic Data Usage). Thus, we have three levels at work here:

- The Data Content Strategy and the Data Usage Strategy are part of the Data Strategy.

- The Data Strategy is part of the Data Management Strategy.

- The Data Management Strategy aligns with the overall Business Objectives of the organization.

Decentralized Data Management – an approach to Data Management in which there is little or no coordination of concepts or standards around the organization and in which different parts of the organization define and execute their capabilities independently.

Federated Data Management - an approach to Data Management in which concepts and standards are defined centrally but implemented locally.

Gap Analysis – Given a documented *Current State* (q.v. above) and a documented *Target State* (q.v. below), a Gap Analysis identifies those capabilities that are present in the *Target State* but absent from the *Current State*.

Guardrail - any document that is used to direct, mandate, guide, or control the implementation and operations of Data and Data Management-related practices.

Guideline - **Recommended best practices that: 1) Support implementation of a standard or interpretation of policy requirements; or 2) address areas not covered by existing policy documents.** Compliance with a guideline is not enforced. (*)

Holistic Data Governance - Data Governance that is aware of both the needs of the organization as a whole and as the sum of its parts and that establishes firm guardrails to ensure consistency across the whole organization.

Line of Business – see *Business Unit*.

Line of Defense – see *Three Lines of Defense.*

Logical Data Domain - **A logical representation of a category of data that has been designated and named.** Data Domains are not physical repositories or databases. Instead, they are logical categories or groupings of data that are deemed important and necessary to a firm's normal business operation. Data Domains include both internally generated data as well as externally acquired data. Examples of Data Domains might include product data, customer data, trade data, pricing data, index data, and risk data. It is imperative that these strategic categories of data are identified, defined, and inventoried to ensure their proper maintenance and use throughout the organization. (*)

Metric – an objective measurement of the current state of some activity of interest to some part of an organization or to the organization as a whole. Key Performance Indicators (KPI's) and Key Risk Indicators (KRI's) are common types of metrics.

Operating Model - **A model representing how a business process or set of processes delivers value to its stakeholders.** (*) This includes the definition of various types of structures that will support the activities of the Data Management/Data Governance function.

Operating Unit - **The level of the organization that performs unique business and/or control function activities.**(*) This is a general term that refers collectively to Control Functions and Business Units.

Policy - **High-level directive that expresses goals and represents management expectations for legal, regulatory and/or organizational requirements.** Policies are aligned to the Principles. (*)

Principle - **A statement of belief or foundational concepts that provide guidance for decision-making and behaviors.** Principles may originate from the organization, legal or regulatory sources. (*)

Procedure - **A low-level step or task in a process that specifies how to achieve an activity.** Procedures are more granular descriptions of steps within a process. (*)

Process - **A series of steps that, when executed in order, achieve a desired outcome.** (*)

Project Management Office (PMO) - **An organizational body or entity assigned various responsibilities related to the centralized and coordinated management of those projects under its domain.** (Source: Project Management Institute (PMI) definition for Project Management Office cited as a synonym for Program Management Office). (*)

Project Plan - Specific step-by-step instructions for implementing a capability. The plan should show resources, expected start and end times, allocated funding, and appropriate oversight.

Roadmap - A high-level schedule of when various capabilities are expected to be implemented or enabled.

Rules-based Control – a *Data Control* specified as a sequence of unambiguous, objective instructions that can be easily interpreted by individuals or that can be readily implemented for automation.

Standard - **A rule or set of rules that defines expected actions for achieving compliance with associated policies.** Standards are audited for compliance. (*)

Strategy – see *Data Management Strategy*.

Target State - A summary snapshot of all capabilities you plan to implement within your Data Governance/Data Management organization by a specified date.

Three Lines of Defense – a framework for Risk Management in which there are three distinct levels of risk oversight. This arrangement is very common in the Banking industry but many other industries use a similar approach, even if they do not use the term "Three Lines of Defense" to describe it. The three separate points of oversight may vary slightly from organization to organization, but the most common implementation is to have oversight:

- At the point of execution (First Line of Defense)

- By an independent monitoring group, such as an Operational Risk Management Control Function (Second Line of Defense)
- Independent Audit (Third Line of Defense)

Vision - A very high-level statement of what the organization desires to achieve over time.

(*) These definitions are from the EDM Council's Data Management Business Glossary (https://www.dcamportal.org/glossary/) and are used with the kind permission of the EDM Council (see Acknowledgements for more information about the EDM Council). The Council's Business Glossary divides each entry into two parts. There is a "Definition," which is the text shown in bold, and "Commentary," which is the text shown after the bold text.

Appendix

A. Guardrail Characteristics

Category	Name	Description	What	Sample Level of Specificity	Characteristics
Strategic	Vision	A very high-level statement of what the organization desires to achieve over time.	WHERE WE SEE OURSELVES	We are a community of data literate information champions.	Aspirational; General; Not Enforceable.
Strategic	Principle	A statement of belief or foundational concept that provides guidance for decision-making and behaviors.	WHY WE CARE	We will always operate in accordance with our code of data ethics.	Foundational; High-level; Not Enforceable.
Strategic	Business Objectives	High-level goals to which senior management is committed.	WHAT WE WANT TO ACCOMPLISH	· To increase our customers' trust in us by at least 15% this year. · To grow sales of <our new product line> by 20% this year.	Directional; Specific goals; Set by Executive Management (the Business), not by Data Management.
Strategic	DM Strategy	A statement of approach and prioritization for how the DM function will support the achievement of the Business Objectives.	HOW WE'LL GET THERE	To ensure consistent understanding of our data, we will establish an enterprise-wide data catalog.	Directional, Aligned to Business Objective; Accountability lies with leadership.

Category	Name	Description	What	Sample Level of Specificity	Characteristics
Governance	Operating Model	How the Data Management function will be structured to meet the objectives of the DM Strategy.	WHAT WILL ENSURE THAT	· We will establish the following hierarchy of Data Governance bodies... · We will establish the following initiatives to grow our data culture...	Structural approach, Prescriptive but at an organizational (rather than activity) level.
Governance	DM Policy	High level directive that constrains how data will be managed to meet legal, regulatory and organizational requirements.	WHAT WILL ENSURE THAT	Comprehensive Metadata must be collected and published for all CDE's.	High-level but enforceable and auditable. Mandatory compliance.
Governance	DM Standard	A rule or set of rules that defines infrastructure-independent actions for achieving compliance with the DM Policy.	WHAT WILL ACCOMPLISH THAT	Within 15 days of establishing any new CDE, the following Metadata attributes must be defined for the CDE (...), approved by the <appropriate committee> and published to the Enterprise Data Catalog.	Specific, enforceable and auditable. Mandatory compliance.
Execution	Process & Procedures	A series of steps that, when executed in order, achieves a desired outcome. A low-level step or task in a process that specifies how to perform an activity.	WHAT WILL ACCOMPLISH THAT	To create a new entry in the Enterprise Data Catalog, perform the following steps...	Highly specific, enforceable and auditable. Infrastructure-specific. Mandatory compliance within stated scope and applicability.

Category	Name	Description	What	Sample Level of Specificity	Characteristics
Execution	Guidelines	Recommended best practices that: 1) support implementation of a standard or interpretation of policy requirements; or 2) address areas not covered by existing policy documents.	HOW WE'D LIKE YOU TO DO THAT	Before entering any metadata into the Data Catalog, you should solicit input from the Data Owner, the Business Data Steward, the Data Architect, the Technical Data Steward and any relevant Subject Matter Experts.	General in nature but may be specific to one or more activities. Recommended but not required. *Not enforceable.*
Execution	Roadmap	A high-level schedule of when various capabilities are expected to be implemented.	WHEN WE'LL DO IT	N/A	Planning document. "30,000 foot view." Dates may be approximate. Subject to change and regular review.
Execution	Project Plan	Specific step-by-step instructions for implementing a capability. The plan should show assigned resources, expected start and end times, allocated funding and appropriate oversight.	WHEN WE'LL DO IT	N/A	Initiative-specific execution document. Contingencies may be built in but the timing should be considered as quasi-mandatory.

Table 10: Summary of Guardrail Characteristics

B. Connective Tissue

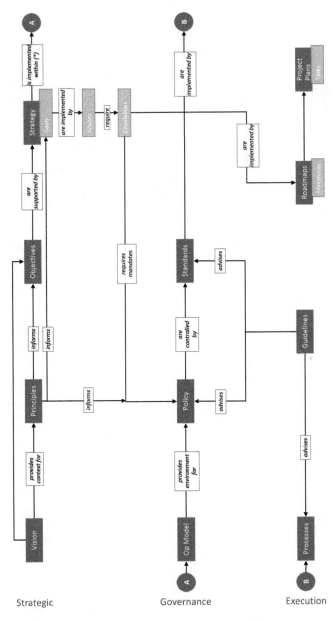

Figure 41 - Summary of Connective Tissue

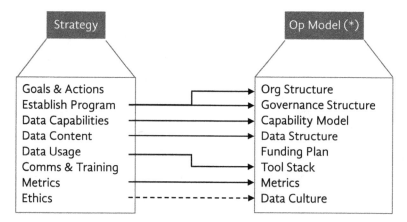

*) In order to more clearly show the relationship between the Strategy components and the OpModel components, the components of the OpModel are in a slightly different sequence here than how they are described in the body of the book.

Figure 42 - Connective Tissue between Strategy and Operating Model

The figures in this book are available for download from the book's website: https://technicspub.com/holistic-dg.

Index